TIME ON THE TURN

By
M.j. Scott (USA)

*Happy Reading
+
Traveling

Love,
Marilyn*

xulon PRESS

M Scott

TIME ON THE TURN
by M.J. Scott (USA)

ISBN 9781498428811

www.xulonpress.com

CONTENTS

Chapter III

TAKE TIME TO REMEMBER

Chapter IV

TAKE TIME TO ENJOY

Chapter V

TAKE TIME FOR THE LITTLE THINGS

PROLOGUE:

The clock devised by intricate process to calculate the seconds accurately. The span of the hands, as it revolves, touches the light and darkness of day and night.

Wheel of living rotates with a momentum that becomes a tempo in times participating turn. Where go these wheels of traveling through life is determined by choice and becomes a destiny in balanced rhythm, or vibrates in discord if negative the response.

Simplicity can be lost in the rush of complexities, yet found in greater magnitude by sensitivity and awareness. Taking time to appreciate the experiences upon the daily role of living brings TIME ON THE TURN into a ribbon of thought. No diary would read the same, no thoughts to repeat, yet experiences shared upon the joys of life like the giant wheel turning in time. Touch of inspiration borne by desire, becomes new eyes to witness the greater dimensions of living.

TIME ON THE TURN invites your thought and the product gained will be your own investment and interest in living. TIME ON THE TURN will continue beyond these pages into journeys of personal remembrance.

M. J. SCOTT

TIME
ON
THE TURN

Chapter I

TAKE TIME TO FIND

SHENANDOAH MORNING

Little stone walls to hold the hillside high, and watch the highway swinging by. Blue-eyed bachelor buttons overlook the hazy valley of morning. Dishes were fashioned to hold victuals and valleys to hold a fortress of strength. Down in the valley beside a Waynesboro Church, a sign spoke so clear. "Thank God, God never takes a vacation."

Leaving Jeffersonian hills behind and traversing a later era's birth. Joining a parkway named for a President too of our United States. Woodrow Wilson Parkway winds across the tops of rolling hills and grants greenery untouched. Right to Verona a town unseen, but before the sign a welcomed sight of weeping willows and shade for a winsome home.

Cars in passing, feature luggage all packed, and children playing in the back. All this as time on the turn rolls under tires revolutions, minds soothing solution and time now to spare.

A garden visited for eyes quick glimpse and beauty tended, cultivated, and growing. Food growing in soil so fertile, flowers blooming in the morning sun and all this in beautiful Shenandoah.

Up ahead Luray Caverns beckon with signs to come find. While people wait for newcomers entrance across the bridge between stranger and relative to meet. A silo like Appollo's cousin and old house matching roof alike. Queen Anne's lace dots the country green, while Victorian farmhouses consider the changes. Little gravel roads grew up and became Interstates of today and river banks slipped past the parlour view.

My Shenandoah Morning winks away into sultry summer, and takes a turn into grey dress of haze. Miniature zinnias place a brilliant period on Shenandoah morning.

A NEW TITLE

Warm, autumn sunshine upon a wind of northern chill. Beside a stream of crystal water, rushing past from children's busy hands at building a knee high dam.

All this has been done before, as generations long have loved this same crystal stream. A fountain that has beheld memories, but the waters are always different. So people come and go, and the 1700's rush into 1800's and 1900's are past the middle of using.

A Fall Festival in the valley between two mountain ranges is a bit of spicy touch of all those years back in the passing. Enter this place and the old steam engines for threshing wheat come chugging to life, by those who have taken the dust and dirt of time from the long stems and unwound the belts for another long pulley of use.

There's a noise like a saw-mill, but it's not so big and strong. It's the way the logs were clutched by man in a vice, and the blade was taught to slice those logs into pieces like long vienna loaves. Perhaps the timber was the age's bread, a place to build, live and partake. And the sawing stops for it has shown us its daily spread.

The copper kettles hold an amber liquid, and apples bobbing in the brew. A long handle with a paddle moves back and forth, around, up and down. Don't burn the kettle with its hours of labor, for each minute passed must have its temperature to boil and boil, stir and stir, add ingredients more, and find again a day has made such apple butter you could never buy with a label—other than home-made and canned with strong heart and hand.

Did we forget to tell of the hickory fires, and charcoal smoky haze rising toward the maple trees that were painted for just such an autumn day? A Festival among the trees of colors, and the skies so high in azure blue. Did we forget or were we ever told how sugar cane was ground, horsedrawn round and round and squeezed by a press to make a green substance far from a pancakes plate? But put in a vat, like a copper maze of pans going up and down, heated by another fire, and cooking slowly until out of a small funnel pipe it came, dark liquid for a daring taste bud to eat.

A hominy maker with a heavy wooden machine, with belts to make it grind, and how it's done must really take time.

The cider grinder like an organ grinder who turns his wheel by hand and wipes his brow as a cup is filled. This is the way apples become liquid and seeds become ground. Far from the mechanization that clear apple cider is bought upon a grocery shelf. It's an amber look, like the apples may have found it hard to make up the skin and rind in a season, and be crushed in many turnings and become a branche's liquid in the churning, churning mill.

So strong these hearts to teach another generation of how the daily work became a year's own pride, in the generations having slipped into time. And we savor for a moment in the home-made kitchen, what must have been true gratitude for the food prepared from the growing land. Placed upon the table for such a spread—the hungry had worked and earned this moment of weariness into blessing. Once upon a time brought back again.

6

Touch the work of thimble and hand, of the crafts that lay upon the tables not so much in admiration or may I buy, but to show how time spent upon the needle well, can bring such beauty of heart into the eyes of beholder's praise.

Precious people, with fingers bent, but eyes glistening in their work. Little ladies, sewing more scraps for the beautiful loom, that makes a rug a story book of color and memories for a hearth, and for feet to walk upon in gentle thought.

A broom that has come from tree, field and man's own craft. A day into minutes, it seemed to be—watching him bend this of nature's growth into a broom that could keep the dirt from near the door. How often do we stop and wonder, at the beauty of such honest hands, bending, forming, molding, and sewing nature again into man's use and need, and appreciation?

Step into a room filled with life—some upon recorded paper, some upon a book's open page, and more upon the faces of those who hold the past in high revere.

To mention names would forget so many, and to forget even one, would make a knot, loose the design upon a woven bit of history. The beauty of it all, carrying the years in the past, so gently along. Could we but go back and touch the one who made a quilt for all six sons? In the 1800's this came to be, and hear a lady tell of a piece of paper she saw but once, of a family name from the ship's log of the great 1700's.

What has been lost? The time to tell it all, and fragments of this day has been given for us to fathom but for a fleeting time, and wonder if preserving it in a continous flow, like the crystal stream in the inheritance of us all. Or is it but for a few, and somewhere inheriting the kingdom seems to be not for the meek, but for those who seek to carry it from beginning to the end.

Festival of the creating, working, loving heart, this is more than an autumn bubble—it is reality in the flowing current of life. A New Title has become festival in autumn perfection—A TIME TO REMEMBER.

SUNNY ESCAPE

A ripple of thought carrying foam away, and splashing falls, years age youth, and yet today. A silver thread from spider's web is touched by sun and dried too soon. Where can you find this idyllic place? Come along on a journey of thought and find uncle's rushing stream.

Leaving the fast rolling Interstate pace—that cloverleafs through cities anxious design. Cross over bridge and turn off into a State Highway well maintained for all. Just off to the left and through a small town noted advancement, culture and progress—Bridgewater so well the name it implies in the Shenandoah Valley beneath Skyline's view. Find the turn out of town and fork in the road brings state to county and into farming country by lane.

Just gravel by now and find a mailbox with a familiar name. Limestone rocks to set off the turn with blue bachelor buttons. A bridge over water with boards sharing view of the creek, and mushroom castles on buttments beneath. No barnacles here or ocean foam, or populated masses surface to shore. Here on the bridge just about noon, children to play in clear creek moving. Wading in glee just like father's youth before.

There on the hill high above the road, hums a happy homestead that weathers storms and shines on. That white fence surrounding sets it off from the world as welcoming those who love to return.

Return with maturity bringing youth at their heels, all family comes to find this mansion among the hills. Mansion

9

of memory, dreams and peace where rivers flow, hills watch and sycamore blow. Rocks are worn by child's own play, weathered by time's continual flow, and embedded firm for landmarks to remember again.

What marks have you left to find your way? Footprints fade, notches heal, and maps change. But memory indelible with sheer delight never fades so far that renewal isn't available. Call of the world success in it earned, return to the land, family, "kith and kin." What joy to have come without an invitation at all. Where can you go with no announcements given? Few if any, the answer of etiquette at all. But believe and find that life grants this too—at a bend in the road of golden experience.

Time on the Turn so much you bequeath to those who live as free as the land, butterfly and Thee!

THAT SPECIAL PLACE

Let view slip through the curtains and meet the early dawn and fog. The meadow has been in a sea of gentle mist and now the day beckons it to hurry. The dew still lingers and the sun catches a topaz drop upon a blade of sodden splendor, and there it dances suspended between the lips of night and the throat of day.

The hill is still here, that hugs the bank in a gentle slope and lets it slip into the stream and choose its own pace of journey, and height to move. Traces show the water rises in a storm and slackens in the need, and like the lazy soaring hawk, today its gentle in its movement, unhurried in its pace, and in this special place it speaks the same kind words of "walk slowly" don't miss a sight, or fresh new autumn scent.

Nature is blessing this world of autumn in review. Look at the trees come amber in the glow of late morning sun. Like a breath of a red spray the taller trees have caught this splatter and green begins to nod into a new array.

Some giant snakefeeder winged in flight hovered near like a helicopter and by its own control disappeared across the bank. High on the hill the corn is still in its fodder and pumpkin orange would make the color stand out against evergreen and fence. The sheep graze up the hill, in slow munching movement, and watching is a stationary tree in outstretched desire to grasp it all.

To be here, is to be living a life, needed and to be appreciating the winging of all humanity and nature in a blend of realities hold.

11

Can you take a moment and find a place to watch the beauty of this singing world in focus? This special place is where I check my focus, perspective and dreams into goals that have been realized, new ones designed and some that are unknown even to me.

Is the unknown like an unspoken song, its rhythm may be here, but the words are only in the creating. The creating can be done and the place may be its own name found.

This special place—do you dare to search it out, or are you there and never noticed its presence before? Its name is heaven made, and spirit knows when it has been found. Are you at home or far away—I can not say!

This Special Place!

FIRE LIGHT

Beneath the sycamore gaze the fireside blaze rises, and smoke rings curl in whirling, swirling circles. Licks of fire, ragged, jagged and slender, bend around the logs in hungry hurry.

The evening stirs aside only to welcome a bit of fog that comes up the valley from its resting place along the Shenandoah mountains. The little stream that keeps its path beneath the run away hillside has its own evening echo.

But for a moment this writer is alone to listen to the fire clicking its eager tongue, the stream singing its own fresh thought, and a late to bed robin calling from the maple, then the walnut tree and coming by for a last look at today.

At the brow of the hill just above a branching apple tree, that is the only orchard sentry remaining, stands a darkened house. It's empty except for memories of its children it sheltered, gave some afternoon playtime shade and now its only resident is a big roly-poly groundhog. It's a touch of old Virginia mountain nostalgia that gives a venetian blind effect. A little glimpse, a quick brush aside and gone are the slow and unhurried moments that used to wrap this side of heaven in remoteness.

Change of the times from window size and house—chimney, porch and swing that gently gave its own touch to the picture. Words can scarcely beckon thoughts so far back that hunting dogs can be heard and a fox hunt or raccoon chase can be revisualized. But here in this niche of America tonight each of these sounds, sights and philosophies are clearly etched.

Sparks that could rekindle a fire if settled into a dry bit of tall grass, lifts its light like a firefly bright and gently glides but for a moment and gone. The night is no longer alone, and the winging bats play chase at treetop height. Have they slept in the deserted house all day, and will suddenly scare the evening like a dropping log upon the fire which just raced my heart?

Little crickets and frogs join the oratory of vanishing twilight and seem to know now it is their own part to speak. A wayward lamb gives out a bleat or two, and call again for its Mother's soft nose to feel. The romance of summer seems to fit this place in it's loveliness and so often unheard hum. Slip your thoughts into the evening and the crackling fire sends silence away. Smoke fills the air and the aroma is neither cedar or pine—its own blend of a wood and aging tobacco kind. Like an old favorite pipe a silent visitor might have enjoyed, the fire has its own comfort, and my vigil is the right kind of blending time.

Retreat to the mountains and "I will lift up mine eyes from whence cometh my refuge and strength." Dare we be so bold as to come again for this medicine rich for the soul? Campfire of evening, sonnet in the countryside quiet, and blue haze of mountains disappearing, but always here tonight, tomorrow and forever.

Voices, happy returning, reminiscing, and life is a sharing of joys.

COUNTRY SUNDAY

Wide open windows of the heart of church, and as "kinda' hot" creeps across the worshippers' lips, a soft mountain breeze moves in the midst.

Across the silence, waiting for the Sunday School teacher, some seem uneasy, but the refreshing silence—the ease of tensions is a beauty in recognition of silent worship. The tiny white cabbage butterfly darts to and fro above a fence row, and seems like our hurrying hearts before arriving.

The lesson begins, and a lovely lady dressed in blue, and crowned with grey, says, "the way they live is more than what they have." The Ten Commandments of God given to Moses —they will never be changed or repealed, recorded in Exodus 20. Basis of peace and prosperity of all people—"no man breaks God's Law, he only breaks himself." The towering commandments are being studied, the teacher with a book in hand holds answers in the palm and questions the listener. Suddenly the teacher becomes the proclaimer, and the listener becomes the challenged. What if a question was asked directly and this mind had no answer? Will God ask the questions like an examiner and the examinee become lost for answers? Will the test be question and answer for eternities destination? Or is the living test a daily testimony won or lost, forgiven and each day a new beginning?

Sitting amid a silver haired circle of believers and I feel like I'm in the midst of living angels and yet they don't know their strength and power of witness.

Questions of the lesson rise as high as the mountains, and suddenly a tangent throws the listener down the mountain like the tablets of commandments and the long climb back to the summit of thoughtful worship suddenly has so many lines of swelling communication. Overworked brain waves interfering with spiritual waves of communion. Could these listeners realize that suddenly their natural experiences return and leave the lofty learnings to a moment in the past?

He has walked here, across the meadow, touched even a buckhorn weed and made it lovely in the sun. The fresh wind of Sunday, the song of birds, and voices of the Sunday School mount and this hour trickles away and a new week dawns.

THERE'S A CREEK FLOWING

A bank of green slips across the hill with tree roots hidden from the view. Rows of trees so summer green, and fresh renewed from a taste of rain. Branch, trunk and tree stands in dark effect above the creek flowing free. Storms swift announcement created change and waters choked in heavy silt.

Night stilled the waters feverish course and gentleness of morning brought beside still waters clear. Along the bank, among the trees, reaching out to meet the bend and turn on around. Slipping past sycamore roots sipping a drink at the pause, and bend to the sandbar on the course. Storm cut loose the anchored roots and built bridges with fallen trees. While morning healed the angry changes in bobwhites meadow talk. Chant of the birds along the valley, and cowbells tinkling refrain, brings human wakefulness that a new day is beginning.

A walk to the creek, away from the hill beside pastures and fold. Catching the sound again "beside still waters" and remembering too, "Thy rod will protect me."

Arch of the branches, crease of the white fence all waiting man to rise and walk his day. Stationary the fence, while world turns its course, tree stands and waits for winds retort. And waters never ceasing until man drains it dry. While man quenches thirst by the physical effort, and moments like this when spiritual seeks release.

Wake up, "oh people" on solar track and seek quiet places where there's time for the next turn. There's a creek

17

flowing within the heart. Experiences of life fill its channels to flooding, while if time for a recipe of living would better give proportion, dimension and peace.

Heart of the creek is endless and moving, heart of man can be lifted too. Crush of the ant, work and time—impedes outlook, higher vision and meditative thought. While a still small place of hidden retreat brings walls to withdraw and life to reopen.

World, Time and Man on the turn, while there's a creek flowing free, boundless as the heart, full as the life, and precious to man—it's the Soul.

RETREAT IN RHYTHM

Dear Lord, how do we become a part of your great rhythm—life?

Besides fresh waters that have no time for the past, as they rush into the future from the now of living. There goes a chant as light as a butterfly, as gentle as water crossing a rock all smooth from wear, whirling like a cup and spilling on toward the great gravity of its urging call.

A footbridge only inches above these waters there's pure peace in these urging calls. The water surges in great splashing gurgles and washes the weariness away from the entire being.

Where do you find these places that are of hallowed saving? A little way from the mainstream of life these little branches cross stones and earths great foundations and here amid the shading from old walnut trees kind tending and sycamore's gentle waving-there is peace.

A page slipped away in the wind, dropped into the water, hurried under the bridge, rippled in it's call to cross the rocks, up, down, sink and then gently glide just beneath the surface. Is life like the page, caught in the wind, dropped into the waters of hurrying on, up, down and sink in many experiences? Or are we able to gently glide?

Follow that paper, no, I'll stay here and let it find its chosen course, for it's free to leave, and I'm free to choose, and for a moment longer this valley and its waters; this valley and its morning winds; this valley with its lush meadows, like resting against a creek and it's held so kindly by a tall grassy bank.

Down in this valley, the birds sing for their own sweet release and joy; and for all of these of nature's gifts I give great thanks.

Sunny Sunday beyond the shade, and the water catches the brightness and glistens in a sparkling reverence. These waters flow from a mountain's heart and a fresh spring that has the taste of "the good gifts" of God's Handiwork.

"Thy Kingdom Come, Thy Will Be Done," beside these waters the promises seem so clear. Beside these waters unstilled by man, but in the heartbeat of eternity's call.

Last night's fire seemed but ashes in the smoldering, but there's a flame that has been fanned by the breath of hope. Breezes change direction, thin smoke but a small blue haze and it's the past being but a warm memory. The waters so tingly cool, are the voices of today promising all we are willing to seek and to cherish.

"To live and to honor"—vows of our lives toward our Lord who walked this way once and can be faintly sensed in these moments of reverence. Everyone has gone away, for a little while, and they gave me the greatest gift of all. Seconds to be found, minutes to be caught and found so grandly once again in peace.

Peace beside the rushing waters, they rush not too fast, nor ripple too slowly—but constantly moving by, just like the time of our lives. Crystal clear these moments, more precious than the gems upon the hand, these can't be stopped, but oh so greatly enjoyed. Across the stones, all different in colors, and aren't you thirsty too, for just such a retreat? Retreat of the body to a restful place, and it's here in the hidden valley, between these mountains, blue, and high and beautiful, the Shenandoah and the Blue Ridge—how we love your beauty.

Everytime we return, you become our deeper strength and the peaceful valley, the winds of summer blow so quickly away.

Retreat—but please be here when I return. Please be the same for another bit of heaven's open view. Knocking at the door a picture of entering in—this is the inside of the heart and it's fresh and happy again.

Welcome Home whomever comes—but you must care for it to understand its rhythm.

HONE QUARRY

Country round the Virginia roads, winding up the mountain. While "kith and kin" speak of times reminiscent where stories lift so high. Where the 26's of 1900 drove model T's, that climbed and chugged up to Hone Quarry. Where bears were chased and horses hitched to rail and post. Days ago an evening fun of pitching horseshoes by lantern light. Fjord the creek in yesterday, but rocks remain now beneath the bridge.

Chat returns to Uncle who came up in horse and buggy. Washed rut roads let rocks bruised crust break through. One time wild turkey spied on the ledge is brought again to re-membering eyes.

Look for the "hone" now covered by an earthen dam— when used at time for razors sharpening start. Hone the Quarry is an era covered, while metamorphic changes con-tinue. An old rail fence walks away out of sight and the old road lumbers up through the hollow and the 99 year lease is gone. Climbing up to Reddish Knob where sun warms the fire tower tall. Above the mountain ridges the forest exudes a perfume surpassing Chanel.

Camp roads shadowed in coolness along the George Washington National Forest. Graves of early settlers marked beneath a towering oak. Passing a forest plantation of red and white pine marking the 30's advancement.

All from Hone Quarry, to a mountain top trip and re-turn. Return to home from Quarry run, and storm has brought the mountain down. Wind on the roof, and rippling trees while fallen in the creek and no longer crystal clear. Muddy the water beneath the bridge, while crystal thoughts burst after the storm. Raindrops fall and Hone Quarry returns to memories precious case.

HONE QUARRY
Shenandoah Mountains

BRANCHES OF ABRAHAM

At Narrow Passage a turnoff brings another event in time to mind. Watching the fog over skyline changing with lift and fall.

Families, smaller today grew from solid stalk and transplants from Old World surviving the change. Old World individuals sought to bring with them traditions well rooted and filled with strength. The unit called "family" had a male figure for central authority and like a giant to carry decisions affecting all. So the dynasty brought strong men and their wives, the best of the fittest and she could do man size work. Hands well lined with wrinkles like strong timber. The woman met the old figurehead in authority and was accepted to stay or unfit and go away. Thus a patriarch grew, a clan became and well born the size of families grew. Young men brought again their women for acceptance and now larger grouping seemed to vote for approval.

Passive woman reached greater approval after giving birth of sons and daughters, and after rearing these youth to maturity. Then moving out from under heavy work and responsibility these women could then stand beside husband and survey the larger clan.

The older generation passed on the unwritten empathy, traditions and spirit of unity. The Old World now successfully established took its place beside the church in dominance. Each representing stability, and continuation for perpetuation.

Follow through the generations into three and four removed from the central figure. The land called these families and higher mountains to cross, thus mobility brought another transition. So homesteads represented a new frontier linking the mountain separating. Into the midwest from eastern land and the unity remained in the hearts of the traditional bred.

The Dynasty of Clan now had several in authority and women had children, and they grew into another generation to be taught. Church brought education and colleges replacing the family elders teachings. The individual became aware of their own qualities and began to trek into freedom of thought. The family branches reaching out toward following their own sun. So traditions leave only the living but set by the ancestors into written upon the heart.

So relatives numerous and mountains between. Cities and roads all springing ahead and now bringing those out of isolation and into easier communication. The unity returns for reunions and memories to review. Old albums come out of parlours and photos exchanged, while wide-eyed small folk wonder who's that in riding habit? Or who's embroidered velvet settee? So the inbred yearnings of heritage returns to glimpse upon the now recorded ancient sepia toned photos. Writings in personal autograph books all covered with wine velvet and beautiful old style English script. Recollections of poetic words to convey emotion now colorful speech and ancestors dated.

The generation gap doesn't exist among this clan of kith and kin, for each now accepts those born into its lineage, but those yet joining and renewing the blood are chosen behind rimmed glasses, greying temples, and thoughtful faces.

The Old World and New are living today, but have loosened the lines and allowing the outflowing growth among these families. Great people they have become, America's fine backbone. And now the Dynasty, seems to have sent the continuation into the hands of Our Father God.

Time on the turn, wheels under this motion and emotion is captured among the misty mountaintops of thought, heritage and old fine name. A good name is to be counted finer than gold and the whole world over, heritage to be so eloquent and worth preserving.

Crossing Abrams Creek, and all stock from the lineage of Abraham.

A SONNET TO VALLEY WAYS

Winds of another day, blow across the Shenandoah Valley and time speaks of its own retreat beneath the gaze of mountains eye.

Bees hum their summer song and let the log cabin's open door become their entrance and a cut out window which has no pane their fast exit sign. The hand hewn logs have wrinkles and notches of hands hard work in years gone by. The wasps have found a fortress to attach their adobe homes like Capistrano's own swallows nest.

A dried up stream bed matches the old cabin where it too has lost its moisture and has weathered. Limestone outcroppings have lines of abrasion—scratched by time. Last fall's leaves lie scattered like tiny far flung scraps of yesterdays design.

To walk this land that man made his own as the signature has been embossed and the sprawling fences show neighbor to neighbor how far it all extends.

An underground spring surfaces in the shade of an old sycamore and drifts into a rocky dish that holds it clear and smoothly silent. A limestone rock shares a corner of paradise with moss so green that an artists brush can only make in replica.

A worn out stone may have been an Indians own maize and grinding palette, while a song of summer breezes smile at all the flickering tones and thoughts.

Time stands still for such a few idyllic moments of reverie, but these exist and the aged is mellow and handsome in the refining of time—could we?

A wormy chestnut corner post where fence is securely anchored, the gnarl is an open eye for a woodpeckers entrance and a courageous hand.

The sky is dotted in white powder puffs of a child's carnival of cotton candy but here amid the bobwhite's call and mockingbird's voice it has the forming urge for showering blessings galore upon the day.

Wild pink stars have reached up like a bouquet beckoning for a hand, but not to change the ecology, only by a words small rippling splash and gone.

Clever little rooster in his barnyard picture frame chuckles at the afternoon intruders, but rather proud to have been noticed! He flies to the top of the fence and proclaims his kingdom's grand crow to fame, but disappears like a dandelions feathered crown.

Footsteps across the pastures claim a few blades of grass and drop low, but the tall spearmint is promising to be cool and if it's snipped will multiply another summer day.

Can days multiply while hours seem to be refreshed in shade of the wind's own repose?

MICHAEL'S VALLEY

WALK AWAY TO HOME

Home from the work, home from the day, home to all. Carry he a loaf of bread along the highway facing mist and spray. The city lies far ahead but out here where no suburbia eats away. Home past a wide lake of fog above the water. Fishermen two, row a boat like silent creatures of The Owl & The Pussycat!

Home toward the west, home now for rest. Table is spread with a tray of bread, cheese and salt to lift the hunger. Wipe away the tray, there lay bread not from a storybook tale.

Rain splashes down on the cinderblock and empty the arms of a plantation mammy. Stand tall beside the road, across the machines are steaming from today. Away from the ground where peanuts were first planted, away went the men.

Markings along reclaim history by Battlefields plaque, and turnpike signs hurry on past. Here in Dominion, old by settling days and so new to those who have just arrived. Raindrops and fog fall tonight on the man walking home. Home just past the raindrops and fog, and on into the setting sun. Home with the loaf of bread and no servant was he. Home under the clouds of heavens comforter, fleecy white as a veil of cotton. Gone the cotton of this field, gone the small nuts that grew here too. Walk on by, oh man of the road, you own the whole view of world if you so can see. So today oh man of day, and oh man of moon, shared this moment and touched. Yield right of way the travelers heard.

Last exit before entering toll road, merging traffic, man with the loaf of bread can not pay. Is this like us of fast the living, read signs and move on? Well never heeding signs until stop is the limit?

Man with the loaf of bread where went you there? Exit 4, Colonial Heights did you go there and lose the way?

Go back to the lake with fog, boat and silence. Return to the cinderblock house still waiting—for home is wherever you make it and made by people who really care.

BLUE STORM

Gum Spring is seven and Charlottesville forty-six, and around the bend on a Virginia Interstate is a blue-black storm. Lightning slivers across the sky and trees stand in almond shape. Black highway ribbons out ahead of the tires and blue-black clouds lie in wait. Gusts of wind lick up a white paper and droplets hit nail hard with sounds.

Wind cuts leaves loose from moorings, while lightning cuts the air into a static instant. Thunder bursts upon lightnings programmed touch and Blue Storm reached maturity. Torrents raced through gulley and stream, and eroded again soil's soft substance.

Blue Storm rolled across hill and vale while Shannon Hill stood in the evening sun. Blue sky and setting sun kissed the day goodnight and watched a tear streaked face being dried with airs return. Sun meets fog and sends a golden ribbon across the valley. Here after the Blue Storm ebbed out of sight, while Zion Cross Roads approached and it seemed that elements of weather and church had spoken.

Could it be that both were formed by ethereal power? Ray of the sun through moistures touch, like funnels of light projected. Blue Storm in minds remembrance.

A GENERAL SETTING

East of Buckingham Court House, doing a country trot would find you at one mile out. There a sign says, "ROBERT E. LEE WAYSIDE," a lovely picnic setting. Back in the woods among benches, trees, a marker notes a speciality. "This stone marks the last encampment of Robert E. Lee and his men after the stand at Appomattox, April 1865."

A great large stone beneath an oak holds vigil to this quiet ceremony of a fallen bird. A broken bottle lies nearby and mocks with cutting edges this secluded nook. No restaurant stands to mark these long past cookfires, but Virginia bacon and fried eggs from my kitchen on wheels is haunting enough.

Does history live in the hearts of men, well maybe not, yet beside the table at silence a restless sentry might arouse!

Kudzu vine climbs just west of town and black angus graze on beyond. The road goes up and down like an amusement coaster in slow motion and thoughts race ahead of the evening lights.

HINTS OF AUTUMN

Great giant "S" curves accented at the bend with leaves in hesitant hue. One tree took her cue and curtsied to the new stage lights.

A mountaineer's porch is ladened with fireside logs, while the cabin home was a neat stack of logs and stucco filling. A gingerbread house of color and cotton candy made up the fog.

Leafy arches loped far ahead and swept past a butcher's outdoor tripod. Up at Big Hollow two silent smoke stacks stood, not a smokehouse.

Pointing the way to North Mountain, within the George Washington National Forest, stood a rack of dried corn yesterday and pumpkins dripping like the gourd shaped raindrops. Lashing, splashing all running toward Cow Pasture Creek.

The mustard yellow fire hydrant beside the motel matched those goldenrod hills at last. Mountain tops capped in soft white splendor, "fog before the snow," the snapdragon called.

Cock of the Walk on a weather vane, fanned dry straw feathers and the basket of hay was a decorators painted delight. While fashions stayed high and dry the umbrella carried more than raincheck in its blackhandled cane.

Lowmoor a sign from exit to the highlands above, and names remain. The grimes-golden apples are lying upon an emerald carpet dotted in rhinestones. While a puppy and kitten wait upon the backporch for a snack before noon.

Little Kate Greenaways come off the hangars and form a line at the school house door. The whole amphitheater begins to gather for another production. The players are assembled and Autumn winds are in ready prelude.

Chapter II

TAKE TIME TO SEEK

ROANOKE ISLAND—THE MAGNIFICENT

Sand as silent as Indians creeping—while heat rushes up and faraway thoughts sweep in.

Cross a small drawbridge at a canal's peak and find the perfect spot to bridge yesterday's and today's wonder. Roanoke Island as a legend in the living, still breathes with a breath of colonists dreams. Sails of England they awaited for a word, while now sails race across the pleasure of waters. Upon a canal, at the bridge of rippling thought—these waters were a colonist's hope, dream and thread between their yesterday of England and their today of hope.

Tall trees stand upon the inlet of quiet and speak of mysteries yet unsolved of a colony lost in a new world then, and a still searching world of today. These lands between the seas in a Sound that feels secure, are now unfeared except by a tied dogs cry, but long ago Indians cry for "give us back the land you tread!" And fear crept up the sides of heart and fort where those colonists dwelt.

Voices in the distance undetectable by the span could be the colonists planning or a boater's voyaging plan.

Wet roots, dry roots upon the canal and inlet's face— like the roots of faith in a country that history finds refreshing in its life. Crickets and tree frogs were once the symphonies of night. The records of today are folk in the sounding gong of somewhere to go—someplace, sometime.

Lift the heart, lift the thoughts and find the footprints of yesterday as close as your own soft step in the sand. Trees lift up branches and cones hold forth new seed. What are we leaving in the transmittance of life, hope and liberty that once blew across this island, and still splashes in life?

Bridges that span thought and hold spirit in the height —Roanoke Island—the magnificent.

ROANOKE ISLAND
North Carolina

ROCK OF AGES

Rock of ages upon a crest, where elevations hum nature's melodies. Rocks flowing like honey drops with wind splashing the clifty falls. Droplets fell against the wind and mist but a soft phrase. White heron feathers upon a slender cloud and mountain peaks met like pictures of the clouds above.

Rocks formed gigantic, and I so small,—all for an age of vision and weathering. Wind and water abrasive against the towering walls but crests that stand in gleaming mica. Tiny blue starlike flowers like a blue net, beneath rocks seeping out springlets so fine. Sprigs of greenery work roots into fragile cracks and endure the comfort of a fortress strong. Moss creeps along the lofty plates of rock and lichen of mountains all lends a picture. Sun against mica shine like millions of diamonds upon a grey tablecloth. All this in the Blue Ridge sun of a June afternoon. Tall pines reaching like a Japanese silk screen toward blue sky above and clouds of white all parasols of today.

Crossing under Devil's Courthouse Tunnel, where superstitions ranged in era of Cherokee and Spirit. Lichen like a coral robe lay draped against an outstretched table. Up among the heights where Old Abe Eagles might have nested, none to see, though heights to soar, all this here on the high Blue Ridge. Clouds cover mountain ranges and lift, like masks of green and grey changing places.

Wild rhododendron purple bursting into lavender, leaves rocks on the mountainside and color seems forever here. Stop above a scene beneath a waterfalls rushing down from the thousands of feet, where rocks of ages were touched and waters flow forth untouched.

A volcanic core left from eons, and a rock dome shape with a green growth overhanging. Overlook ahead upon a rocky cliff called, "Looking Glass Rock," and recognized by man that rocks came long before B.C., A.D., and when the foundations were formed. Pisgah Ridge a name from biblical Pisgah Mountain where at heights the Bible too has granted namesakes.

Skies darkening, foreboding the greys, and rocks and clouds seem but to burst, fall and throughout all ages the elevations have kept these secrets. Fresh fern adds her fan like bow and maples too are leafy silent.

Rock of Ages set in stone upon the old church built. These rocks hewn from a fortress of strength into walls to hold physical structure, spiritual dwelling and unto everlasting—THESE ROCKS OF AGES to never cease!

FIVE MINUTES BY THE RIVERSIDE

Five minutes or eternity—peace here beside. Where butterflies dance above waters babbling and gentle falls race by. Crystal clear the water, above pebbles color beneath. Each share nature's treasures and flatrock to sit is a solid throne to see.

Fairyland moss covers large rocks of years ,and look like minnow's forest above their rushing home.

Tree limbs and branches reach out to touch the river's busy life, and each living, breathing, a part of God's great now!

Sun flashing, now and then, dots the paper folds. Driftwood graces the angular banks while yellow butterflies race with the current and thought. Crows loud "caw" brings sharp piercing period into thought, then further away they fly like a comma's pause. Trees like inverted exclamation marks and foliage the period beneath. Return them to their position and this to the literary depth. A heel in the water, a toe on a rock, yet where and when the moisture to meet? A stick submerged looks so still, like a quiet painting upon the riverbed. Stones brought to the knee to see and pile them there, and splash when with care? A child's love for this and Thee and Five Minutes By The Riverside, for our memory. Children search for pebbles, writers search for words, but share we here the water's words, and life, and love, and Thee!

BLUE SMOKE

The sun rose above the mountain today and smoke lay touching the top like grey blue. Lighter this day grew on past freeways all fast. Climb around the hill, wind up the road and narrower it became.

Suddenly the terrain became changed from dense foliage into nothingness. Here near Coppertown, a smelter puffed, and the land laid ravished from smokey tongues that lapped up the former greenery. Now parched and red, lay against suns gaze, tear streaked the hills, eroded into a wrinkled tapa cloth look. Bonsai spots of green topsoil rose in view, and needed careful tending to hold its shape near a small house there. The Company Store seemed to own all houses and where were the people that Appalachia birthed?

Up out of the copperfields hot, crossing roads a building, and suddenly Indian names of North Carolina came into view. A lovely gorge followed a winding river, rapids, and clear crystal water with white capped rocks. A wall of fern was a fortress of freshness and silhouettes so lovely against a roadway.

Smokey the mountains, traversing through the day and now at dusk, smoke of a campfire lifts its own signature to a **BLUE SMOKE DAY.**

CHEROKEES
LIVING OCONALUFTEE VILLAGE

Above Cherokee town, there perpetuates a living saga of Cherokee, a nation preserved from two hundred years of remaining descendants. A proud, strong nation, was dissolved by changing of land and guards, but remnants rebuilding their heritage too and proudly live far above poverty's stare, but greater still because each one cares.

No welfare this group, as told beside the "Seven Timbers in the Council Hall," but earned, and land purchased from others hands. A group now growing six thousand five hundred, and registered before the age of one, daughter and son belong. History retold in living actions of squaws stringing beads, now commercial in plastic fiber, replaced by the former shells and sinew strung. Watching a warrior strong and bold, making arrow heads of flint and perfections aim. The bow stick to mark the distance between hunter and sought—all this brings the arrow into sharper point. Women weaving beside a fire, and hickory smoke ebbs up, too alive and real. Homes that were built between log and red sod holds the hunter's game and families pride. The dried food preserved for a winter's hungry day, all this hanging now to bring our memory refreshed. American Indians these are heritage proud, and gain they status upon a fair days labor. Homes that once were visited by Medicine Man and sweathouse each did have, are todays care at the bottom of the hill among Cherokee Citizen's Hospitals too.

Youth, their own speak fine the English language and Cherokee the tongue so native, dying out like fires own

43

embers, until taught at the knee of parents time. Schooled and taught they go some say away, but heart returns to be their own Council's replacement.

The basketry is done the Indian weaving style, but thoughts must be woven and stories reminding, as reeds are dyed in walnut stain. Do hearts return to yearn their ancestry but no superstitions rage, though wild bears prowl across the mountain ridge.

All this so beautifully shown by living the silent actions of work and guide's own story to tell the interpretative role. But stop to talk with each at the end of tour, and you'll find real Americans who live, and work and love the soil too—they are proud to share.

None to compare, come here to see, all of you will fall into thought among Cherokee—Oconaluftee.

CHEROKEE, NORTH CAROLINA

PIONEER
THE OCONALUFTEE SETTLEMENT

Beside the creek the settlers chose to build a home with Scottish-Irish and French—men's taste. The life was rugged, but free it was, generations grew and on up the valley moved. Life became harder, the best land gone and isolation existed in the valley between the mountains.

Mechanization and war has changed it all, and preserving the era is a historical stride. Not so long ago, just a few to us, when memories were built in Ohio country. Grandparents gave these same gifts to parents and three generations in between—from log sleds to replicas now of it all.

Log house, meat shed, wood shed and barn, all this brought to Oconaluftee, to share pioneer lore. Where copper kettles hang by a three spired tripod that maybe a generation ago boiled applebutter spread. Bee hives not visited but in a hollow gum, just like Honey Bear a story event to explore.

Woodchips and hickory essences, left where hung the meat to cure, and aged to be sure. All, along time, while people toiled and all this beside an Indian trail now grown into a path marched by Union and Confederate forces in later history. Perhaps they ate and tethered a horse here at stream and mountain home? Wait to learn, or watch and discern, all this among Old Smokies hidden.

Corn meal ground upon a grist mill, and aromas above a hot fire yielding. Today's America travels faster by far for just a tinge of yesterday's desire. North Carolina, near Cherokee, come someday, and find it all as truth from afar.

THE OCONALUFTEE SETTLEMENT
North Carolina

MINGUS MILL

The arrow points the way we know. Follow the split rail fence toward the rushing sound. Hike up past the mill to the very beginning and catch the millrace at the start.

Above the mill, they divided the waters at a diversion dam. Here at the floodgate the stream, taps off the water to run downhill. Falling water to turn a giant wheel. Shut the floodgate the gristmill to stop. Follow the water down the millrace and it reaches the mill before the feet.

Moss and fern drink the moisture at the rim, and leaves of fall beneath trees of spring, give mulch and aroma to freshness. Air for breathing so crystal clear, air of an era moving picture still living here. Maples young, leaves of sharp form point the way of the millrace and ferns soft bending like a curve in the bank. Trees have toppled here with time, moss is growing in the sublime. A magnolia dipping arms to grace the mood, and birchwood stands like a thin Indian canoe. Ah! "Land of the Cherokee!" How silent your face, now breathtaking the land you walked in gleaming mica trails and garnet schist the gems within.

A ladder built from twin trees and braced with steps between, a ladder to climb the flume so high. At the cribbing a falls swept fulfilled and down a penstock, like a square wooden tower. Beneath the mill a forebay rushes the water to a turbine now, gone the wheel replaced.

The mill comes alive and throbs a heart—a hundred years ago. The white corn grinding into dusty particles. The millstone, a soft buhrstone from France, takes the grains as they fall, and wind around, wind around and vibrate a fine aroma—nutty—old. Wooden the flooring, wooden the steps, notched and grooved from mankinds living weight.

Indians crushed meal between stones, the settlers came and used stones again but hurried the process with turbine. Now, today, the computer age touches a switch that implements the wheels, but thanks to the mountain pioneer spirit, folklore, and ways are preserved without sodium benzoate.

MINGUS MILL
BLUE RIDGE PARKWAY
Cherokee, North Carolina

AN ERA LOST

Sadness rakes these hills where artisans crafted a living and brought originals to be sold. A decade ago, just beyond "Wilderness Road' marked by Daniel Boone, a Craftsman Guild provided an outlet for creative wares. And here among the Blue Ridge Mountains handcarved, and polished stood a black walnut dining suite. No reason why it should wait for our longing hearts to buy. But now today it's gone, and none stands in its place. The craftsman whose life was in the notched fine woods and hewed, is gone too. Died he here, and no one now uses his tools and trade. No one to replace these finer skills, no one with time, no one with this desire, and along the trees to be whet by a commercial machine. Black walnut a favorite, thinning away, as forests shrink and fold. Are these replaced with seedlings or quicker growth from softer woods?

Spinning and weaving beside a rough loom, stood a quaint old lady to chat. Stories of how her grandmother made a fine linen shirt for grandpa once a year. Cling to these memories, cling to these moments, an era has passed beyond the touch or return.

Grass lies mown, white stones outcropping, heat hovers this mountain, and the age old ways of working with ones hands has nearly slipped away. An era lost for the length of time, and mass originals now are commercially the growing style. Where copper dishes look cloisonne like Orientals have made for centuries.

Where have our traditions, and heritages gone? Unless

our hearts fail to visualize the worth now, remaining remnants will soon be in threads and cut.

Rhododendron of June, dark lavender and paling to other shades beneath the sun. Were you so lovely before the era gone, or came you tall and beautiful to ease the sadness of great crafts gone? Wild orange azaleas stand too for the road's passing beauty, and farewell to "An Era Lost."

A red wool shawl for warmth, and skill set among the strands, reminds us still, and thrushes fly away—over the old log cabin and it never looked down. Cascades to refresh and linger of just "AN ERA PAST."

THE CHINESE CHESTNUT GROVE

Wind climbs up the hill and brings freshness mixed with the rain. The broad leafy canopy above the scarred picnic table listens to the tiny voices of drops pouring down. A black ant hurries to his sandy castle home, while the groves sharp sawtooth leafy points are ever bending near.

"Come on Gang!" a father's call, before the rain pours and wets them all. High on Rocky Knob a camper's haven, among these groves, fresh water, fresh air, and fresh new sights. Puzzling, curling the Chestnut Grove, Chinese short the trees stature, and curling stems for pollens hold. Beneath a tree of last fall's yield lay a pod like porcupine that held the nutty hull. Between a step and curbing edge laid a nut all small and a hull all broken. Treasures can be found to tell its full story, without the magnifying glass to evidence a last trace.

A tulip tree in flowering show, no Garden Club to hail its beauty here. Like Chinese Chestnuts they are out among Nature's Garden, and their view is unsurpassed along the countryside.

The wind across the grove today, is lost now upon another terraced setting. And wind around a bend it was sitting in a hollow on a split rail fence.

Goodbye the little Chinese Chestnuts, goodbye the split rail fence, the Parkway, the Mills, good people, and return to the maple lined city streets, stoplights and busy life. The refurbishment of sights for souls growth may it be among the lofty heights, and never like a house falling down.

51

Descend into the valley and leave the highlands for others enjoyment, vacation and belonging to all who love them.

Chapter III

TAKE TIME TO REMEMBER

CAPSULES OF SPRING

Spring takes different shapes and ways to bring her eloquence into being and filling the soul of presence.

Mynelle, so soft and white her glove, wrapped upon the door or mansions before. Mynelle, so sweet, stood by the pillars tall and breathed the air bending around branches, veranda and watching a golden cat purr. Across the entrance she gracefully walked down the sandy path, with steps to break the descent, out amid the pink azaleas and open there a gate. Oh Mynelle, step through and see just what wonder will fill your eyes. Apple green your coat, dressed in woolen dress for warmth, and strawberry curls bouncing with every new step toward a flowery form.

Wind around paths, violets mark the stepping stones and fill all the raindrops from the shower of spring. Willow branches hang like canopies over little lakes where ducks float, swans glide and thoughts ebb toward the other shore. Half circles cross lakes and yellow flowers climb the distance to weave a pattern of loveliness above the water, and lift the view. Bridges are made for special moments to capture and views and place with the capsule of sights all things right and beautiful. Tulips grace the way and lilies of the valley toll their appeal, while purple faces of violets and pansies reveal their own pure loveliness. A gazebo so elaborate in her white lace veil of French iron, holds hands with vines, flowers and time eternal. Branches of redbud, cherry and peach add color abundant and the eye shines amid these gems of spring. Luxuriant the tree, apple blossoms and dreams seem clustered, and bending toward a small hands touching.

All there for the sharing, all there for the breathing of aroma mixed with petals and lilac and accent beyond. Climb all the paths, wind around all the flowers, and tip-toe through the garden just after raindrops and freshness, coolness and growing of a new season is a reward called, "heaven."

Heaven all capsuled in thought, all cherished in memory, and wind swept into eternity. So spring, Mynelle, your lovely gift and close the gate to keep the treasure for another perfect moment before damp feet find awareness, and wind reaches deeper. Then apple green the wrap, leaves the scene for the chorusing birds, and heralding of the SPRING!

MYNELLE GARDENS
Jackson, Mississippi

PILGRIMAGE CHOICE

An honor to be requested and a privilege to be included, another capsule of a southern day to be shared.

Stanton Hall of Natchez reaches out and draws people into her grasp with the charm of an invitation that might have been soothed in soft speech, or engraved like her lovely balcony.

History for all to read upon a library shelf, but more breathtaking than this, a queen still reigns in majesty and graciousness. Her restoration becoming a pilgrimage of devotion and reminiscent of an era never forgotten. Gone are the builders who fashioned her lovely gown of galleries in wrought iron, pillars of great stamina, but the trees stand close to protect her today. The heart of Stanton Hall still pulses with excitement when those who care to come and admire, caress a mahogany staircase, and fall in silence with deep impressions.

Chandeliers holding high the grandeur of craftsman's skills and parlours to welcome with a touch of velvet magic. Little girls dream of becoming queens of a castle or princesses upon a garden walk, and all the Cinderella's for a moment find Stanton Hall and the glass slipper so very delightful.

No mark in words can convey the emotion of walking up these fine old steps and standing on the threshold of yesterday preserved and today appreciation interwoven into a nostalgic and memorable experience.

The priceless capsule reaches out only to capture the moment of beauty and bring desire to travel again into this antebellum country at Natchez, by the Mississippi, and find a living mansion brushed in warm fresh Gulf breezes of spring.

Surely with the invitation to visit her ladyship, Stanton Hall, no reply but a yearning heart could be more eloquent.

STANTON HALL
Natchez, Mississippi

MELROSE

In Natchez by the Mississippi, stands a giant magnolia and vigilant oak to guard the fine estate of Melrose.

Unchanged since antebellum days except by the distance in era and the amber ice tea glass. Rose colored glasses might recapture the rosy days when Melrose' eloquence was unsurpassed. She has weathered the years in the charming grace of a true southern lady gowned in white and lacy balcony around her throat. Giant strands of Spanish Moss cloak the oak and send a spell of mystery toward the closed door.

Magnolias bloom in their own true season, of white pearly buds that burst into waxen petal gloves, set against a satiny green dress. Melrose in April, when pilgrimages set a fine Confederate rhythm to the flowing gowns of young belles. In a short season, the magnolia waxes the final act upon the stage and closes the capsule of precious glowing memory. The Spanish Moss grows longer, more spidery and to hide the sentiments until another spring's blossoming of azaleas, dogwood and wisteria clinging.

As the hot summer summons, Melrose will cling to the humidity and wait for new breezes of fall, and leaves dipping across her short cropped lawns. Winter will seldom find a sprinkle of powdery snow upon the pedestal top balcony. But ah—sweet spring she comes to life. A canvas caught her very portrait and rebuilt her loveliness and grace that holds her high upon the wall in a frame befitting only a queen. That's Melrose belonging to all who love her past, admire her dignity and thank you Natchez for preserving her ladyship.

The canvas scene will never find a museum wall to seal the picture in cold gallery stillness. Melrose belongs now to an artist's heart, a writer's pen, and a chime's serenade at dusk.

The world so big, it's six o'clock and a rosy light will flood Melrose upon the palette, canvas and next my cameo colored home. Not for sale, but in a capsule's special niche. Thank you God, for bringing Melrose back to another's joy. A four leaf clover has been another giant lawn's reward.

MELROSE
Natchez, Mississippi

A TRACE OF MIST

The afternoon shadows begin to gather shape and form solid lines of boundaries between daylight and dusk.

A rippling brook, clear as a crystal bell sent tones of laughing echo up the sodden cliff. Riding into the tree lined aisle that led to Sandy Creek and its lilting song a refrain for the night becoming.

Walking hand in hand, the gravel creaks its raspy accord and small stones become treasures of the walk. A fork in the path was a parklands abandoned track. Up a hill a choice more difficult in footing and found we there history still alive and clinging to the ruts, walls, fern and old tree limbs.

Misty moisture clinging to the green moss covered flora, and spanish moss a gentle touch of mysterious substance. Climbing on a journey upon the trace of time and this is the true Trace, "Natchez" our long awaited footpath hike. Trees, green, green as the spring silently arch across the path from their lofty sights above. Then the path was blocked and time stood still. A timber had fallen only a green day before, but climbing through dense foliage now horizontal the path became.

"The Old Natchez Trace," not for the modern travel, fast flowing a freeway, but step by step, thought by thought, the old footpath once a highway's return—Natchez to Nash-ville—after the great Mississippi's important flow south.

Explorer, Indian, Soldiers too, Settlers and All have

marched this way. We climbed their hills, saw their sights, but ferns and coolness clung to our travel. Pleasure a hike, travel a long way, day after day, there's difference of need, and difference of weight. But for our today, history hiked along the path and our feet never filled their awesome shoes only the awesome sights and here today as our "National Rights."

A historical endeavor to salvage history, heritage and lore, and hold it close to earth's bosom for those who are to walk the way of a fuller yesterday, meaningful today and adventurous tomorrow.

Will future generations, look down from satellites and see the moon glow of our step into space and see again "a trace of mist that lives forever?"

NATCHEZ TRACE
Mississippi

THE MURMURING OF ROCKY SPRINGS

A river's face wears many shades of makeup, and now its clear complexion has soft beige silt and sand the tone. The crystal clear waters, sing songs by the new formed gravel bar now a falls with gravity flowing.

Children finding rocks, agate, petrified wood, quartz, and more, while their talk wonders back to sayings of "raccoon tracks deep here and prehistoric animals before." Special rocks round, and little hole drilled in the center, are our special kind called, "Indian wampum." So hearts are free to climb the banks, or drift with the waters beside, Psalms 23: "He leadeth me beside still waters, He restoreth my soul, surely goodness and mercy shall follow me all the days of my life, and dwell in the House of the Lord forever."

Prayers of thankfulness rise up as before a picnic is partaken of, prepared by small hands that dreamed of a picnic beside a creek. Willows green reach out across the water from the other bank, and a leafy arm of oak touches my shore and its.

Songs of the birds carol their vocal conversations and a Baltimore Oriole came this morning to our front door. The lacy sky overhead is a silhouette of leaves against heaven's door, and world on the move disturbs not this moment.

Sycamore leaves all young from spring's birth a week, while castles in sand are built today and washed by in a rain.

The sunny bank where driftwood and picnic have relaxed in sand, now becomes cooler as the afternoon breeze beckons to eve. Roots of trees, and roots of thou, are all renewing strength here among nature's pictorial blend of sky, sound and in God's Hand we rest in Him. "Thee will I cherish, Thee will I honor," a wedding song, a song of rebirth in a walk among the bright living and peace near the bend in the river.

Winds of the rain are calling us home, but never dampen our memories among this precious hour, song, tree and Thee!

ALONG THE NATCHEZ TRACE
at Rocky Springs

THE MARBLE & THE BRONZE

High above the Yazoo, once the horseshoe of the Mississippi, the battle lines of Confederacy and Union met against the hilltops of Vicksburg. Now marble monuments and bronze men stand this vigil called Mississippi.

Stockade Redan and an infantry of men once marched these grasslands, tangled now with growth, and a century of memory. Perhaps these mounds still hold keys of this earthworks fort—the eternal torch held upon the Louisiana monument towering above the Battlefield in tour.

Cannons placed and an ironwork bridge spans across a canyon wall. No sun drenched skies to make this scene. Saddened skies above grey with misery of an era ago when American blood was drenched upon these hills, each against another's ideology.

A silent mockingbird sits upon a monument plaque. "To the Arkansas Confederate Soldiers and Sailors apart of a Nation Divided by the sword and reunited at the altar of faith."

Missouri's touch of now tarnished angel, standing with arm outstretched from a ship's bow, that the river played a role. Tarnished and weathered, a cannon still stands at the ready as it was then to preserve a belief. Each Union man, each Confederate man, wore a uniform with pride, and today these hills are shared under one nation's flag. They died *not* in vain.

The spring of 1863 to the spring of now, that healing balm of spring binds the wounds, but scars still remain near history's heart. Winds are free, serious bronze faces now silent and a statue on the horizon standing painted like Washington's Monument above the river.

Confederate lines wind around earthworks that now belongs to a historical tour and a Fort Hill is up ahead. High upon a windy hill, bugles seem to echo, and calvary's buglers stand against the wind to call all to harken. So high the pitch my ears ring in ache.

Another bridge and climb up on the Union Hill. There a cemetery's vigil stands Old Glory at half-mast now for another General more recent in name, but gone to answer to another bugler's call.

Yes, the trumpets are resounding yet, and calling all hearts to Unity. Children climb across cannons, screech over hills, and youth have not yet touched the earthly realism of a nation that was scarred and tempered in a old history of its own rebellion.

The peace bells must chime at some other point upon hills of the Civil War. Listen carefully and the tolling resounds against the jungles now spreading growth.

Ohio's cannons cut in marble, and polished, push up in scope and white wisteria drape down to veil a day that closed. Stop at a sign for a driving law, and check our course and advance on towards Grant's Headquarters. Oak Leaves amass a garland balcony, and windy breezes pull the honeysuckle from the forest's hedge and leave a scent sprinkled in yellow and white, small trumpets flow.

Songs of the free, sounds from children that once may

have had ancestors on plantations, estates and the states that became.

Marble and Bronze now it's become more. It's flesh and blood and our very own young America a heritage that brings the sun to our faces, prayer to our lips and faith to our hearts. AMERICA! AMERICA!

VICKSBURG, MISSISSIPPI

SOMEWHERE OUT THERE

At the vestige of Craven's House, high above Chatta-nooga there lies remnants of the Civil War now quiet and still.

Lonely monuments stand in marble, with tall grass of summer, protecting is the vigil. Earthworks surround in winding rhythm, while power lines run straight across, against clouds strong layers. Tension can be sensed of such a day when an era ago was fought a war above the clouds; now clear with honeysuckle and magnolia perfume to soothe the land. This land the same as the sod somewhere else, grass clipped and unclipped, clover holding honey bee's nectar but this lands a vigil that braved a day and lost her valley from side to side.

Terror lay upon the Mountain Lookout and now is often drenched in rain to ease and clouds to erase a tension between our very own States. So high stands New York's fine monu-ment, with sword in the right hand and at left of the heart a flag held higher.

Cannons stand glazed in paint, preservation to retain, an artilleries position. Wheels and spokes, but grease is gone, along with the men who shouldered its load. Hitches lie dormant and splashed with mud, but they too held both men and blood.

Creep away highways in the valley below, so easy to for-get, or ever to learn, in your smog filled lives what proceeded before? History is masked in facts, and campaigns, men's names loose meaning, and time smokes out the memory.

Stand at the foot of a monument so tall and here in its shadow to feel so small. Sun breaks through and alone to be, among magnolia glistening and waxy leaves, white shaped lights glow in pearly surge high on top. Closer still magnolia petals lie like giant plates flurled with yellow centers decorative pattern. The aroma like lemons, the touch like satin and dry leaves blowing in afternoon sun.

Clouds moving past and airplanes in contrast as this age returns and broken limbs of history leave scars to heal and strengthen the very fabrics skin of a nation strong.

Voices are heard, was it a man's command? A whistle, a signal, could it too a summon be? Summons for us who live today to heed the signal strong—divide not our allegiance to freedom, and yield unto no dictatorship.

Climb these mountains, oh you of status quo, and before too late that you never know. Freedom how beautiful, above a green hill, freedom unending with blue sky so high, and monuments to history, you have given all! Blow on free winds on high, and down below you'll sweep on by. Paths become trails, words become reassurance—that life is now and never so fast but what silence can't teach! SOMEWHERE OUT THERE!

CRAVEN'S HOUSE
Chattanooga, Tennessee

FAREWELL MY LAKE

Waters fill my lake beneath the green studded pine ridge. Tears fill my eyes beneath a tiny thin lashes brown covering, and sit I here on blue a rug to say, "Farewell My Lake."

A lake so close and yet never visited. Yet we shared her quiet retreat between bobwhite's call and cardinal's echo. Breathe a breath of summer warmth and send your message clear. Shadows grow longer beside the Japanese magnolia all shapely from a former clipper's touch. The gardenia bush ready to burst its first pearly gift of nature and for man's sheer floral arrangement.

Pine needles drying beneath summers sun, and noise penetrate stillness while boxes fill a van. Boxes hide earthly possessions, yet soul rings out in freedoms release, to move again!

Bobwhite shouts to the afternoon and an ant reclaims a screen's own wire comb. A screeching scrape crosses the washer and concrete beneath. The precious table that held manuscripts to type, homework to do and a dining table's plenty. It's now separated from its legs and bolts, unnoticed until today—because it always stood there waiting for the new.

Traverse rods now empty holes waiting for another's window choice. Waxed floors awaiting their face to lift and dullness to greet. The ant comes closer, a lizard reclaimed its homeland by displacement a year ago. So it goes, all returns to the country of Mississippi, and I haven't changed it neither to come or go. Only to carry away her fresh breezes of the heart, the warmth of friendliness and southern hospitality humming in the ears atuned.

"Farewell my love," a song seems to cling today between my lake, ridge and thee. As if to say greater vistas we've shared and now moments to carry away amid the priceless capsules of life. All lived to be an inspiriation to others, and a happiness glow that I hum now.

Walls surround to only protect, the world outside reaches in and gives so much beauty that only to behold means moving on, and now this we do! The fireplace is spotless from springs farewell to winter. The visitors of summer swifter than an arrow live by the chimney walls and fly the blue sky free.

Farewell my lake, my house, my friends, but hum I here, to see thee there on another day. Seasons pass and paths we cross, but farewell my lake I'll remember you.

APPALACHIAN GREEN

Color punctuated with happy songs on a morning in spring. Moments like this memorable as precious jade of expensive hues. Green, green the colors of the Appalachian hills and countryside, such a pleasure to lift the eyes to elevations aloft. Breathing air so fresh from days before of hydraulic fluid and jet blasts. This is "leave for military few, and vacation" to those of you.

Hills that bend, blend and climb like slide rules too. Tall crosses against green hills and sky, show the electric spark, to light these parts.

Fort Payne, Alabama, coming soon across where Sequoyah lived in Indian Village now abandoned, and educated the mind to devise the Cherokee alphabet. Symbols that brought enlightment of intellect, like T.V.A. projects, to the lighting of physical abode. All this is scan across history and road, all this to learn and share its appreciative role. Climb every mountain, a song of free expression, and heart leaps to joys certainty.

Clouds above cover, like a soft grey persian umbrella, and sun yields a soft silver reflection. A mirror in reverse shapes the grey into clouds and pines into cathedral spires.

Appalachian our traversing travels and sedimentary its long geological age. Wind, rain and winter's freezing sting, crumbles these hills into etched valleys. Wind of this hour leaves the leaf to wave farewell, and rain to come will wash it back. Candles growing tall upon pines strong spine, shows growth and age reaching another ring in maturity. Appalachian candles, chains and lines, all this with green and envy none.

All this before an exit, all this and return, all this in life's vivid picture. Whistles of a perfect tone, blending this all into a thirsty mile or two.

Chapter IV

TAKE TIME TO ENJOY

GARDEN OF MORNING

At the top of the world in which we live there's a fresh cool morning to find a welcomed sight. Garden of Morning touched only by dew and the approaching sun. The glories of morning quick to rise, from shadows of night to dawn and light. Trumpet vine climbs a white fence and journeys far upon its way. Red trumpets herald the leafy stem and wink to the blue of the morning glory. A spike of glads points to better height above the marigolds and a hammers knocking. Phlox nod and turn their heads and five pointed stars seem to twinkle in a lavender pink gown.

The petunias so white, so large have no elegant perfume to add to the garden, but those ruffles abounding still cry out to be admired. A rock garden standing along the edge has marigolds golden as sun at set, blazing now and a throne for a morning mosquito. The white fence rambles past the vigilant oak in her waxen green satin dress, while orchestras are sounding out the wheels of day. A saw whines as its house to build, and a tap of the bell, a train awakening the rails.

The roses that stand in dewdrops so perfect, while Mother Wren leaves her nest of eggs to approach a feast. The evergreen of the wrens fine house this day, while blue roofs and skies seem to cover a smaller shadow. Blackeyed susans are not so perky today—wonder what their tired eyes are saying as petals fall? The purple asters, a teacher's joy, stand uncut this morning as key to the garden is held untouched. The chrysanthemums a favorite, in all shades of cluster, while sizes and fringe seem all perfection. Crisp the leaves of this fine clump, and grasps the heart at the edge of Autumn.

77

A wee small bunny still lives in the garden and munches more than the Gardeners wish. Creeping past the red geraniums that are signs to hurry and danger there. A carnation bud and leafy salad would feed the bunnies famished taste.

A soft splash falls from the drain spout as dew of the day melts and falls away. White gravel crunches at a footsteps motion, and birds fall silent when Garden of Morning becomes too loud.

A few petals falling, another misty vision, and Garden of Morning remains uncut, untouched, but heart of the Soul has been touched and a portion left as all in a season must be.

JUST A YESTERDAY AGO

Voices ringing with the call of spring, harsher than the cardinals call. The whistle of a bobwhite shriller than the wren.

Sunshine mixed with bleachers, wet wood grain and grass. Wild onions green at a glance like a fields first promise. The tree frogs and bullfrogs all chorus a strange tenor range and purple flowers wild, grace the table of earth. Fast the soft air races across face, field and quiets the little sphere of our own. Mind to fathom, so great a treasure, wealth of lands texture, grasses blade of shape and shade.

Tiny moss so small a magnifying glass would enlarge, but painted on the earths brown fresh canvas, and fragrant the mixture.

A tiny black ant went borrowing for breakfast and found a red bud just his size for dessert. A patch of moss green, so velour to the touch, and creeping away at a snails small pace.

Little crevices of erosion from a raindrop that melted and met another to flow on by the roots of grass. Blue stars touched finger tips that chose the blue throat like vases and caught the dew. A lake hidden, blended color and ridge to hide its size and an old swimming hole it might have been.

A hikers paradise crossing from goal to goal all on a day in Spring and the Swallows of San Juan Capistrano remember their mission too!

SWEET POTATO NIGHT

Came upon a story lingering on the tip of a sweet potato leaf. All the veins of thought filled to near bursting edge. The curl of the leaf and shape of a heart this is a sweet potato story.

On the edge of town lies a rural land, dug, hoed, and loved by its owners. Here the soil dark as night is loved for its beauty, smell and blessings. Plain and Fancy points a sign but pass on by, for no frills at all is the aim.

The highway slick with rainy showers, and tires whistling its own slurring sound. In this fast scene on the edge of a time a horse drawn buggy flew along. The clips and clops of the sharp shoed creature, sleek and fine with the buggy behind. Bearded man home in the rain, to family three and on toward six-thirty. Fresh the air mixed with a tinge of twilight made a hue like the new green on a sweet potato.

In country lanes the buggies flew and open ones for a courting two. Wing of a second and past they flew, and drew on around a curve or so. Courting teens with smiles and pride, while back behind came Grandfather Stern.

Amish country and Mennonite too. Both so close that a tourist's eye finds difference little, and no time for doctrines study. There too no leaf the same, except the stem. And houses stand in blue green window blinds with curtains none. Symbols of worldliness lacking too, when telephones, television and utilities no charge.

80

The uncluttered horizon, unchanging between roofs shape and corn tassel. Hearthside music and dining pleasure brings thoughts of hands preparing the fine fare. Strong hands, fragile the smile, unbleached her face and shining hair. Fresh as the sweet potato in the window there.

People traveling this country of long tradition, spare its fragile moment suspended between retention and submission. Sweet potato night sharp edged, veined in lines, and heart shaped in perfection. Fresh untouched, lovely and innocent as the three lassies pushing the cart of bread from hearth side to a waiting truck. Young and happy as the courting teens, wise and stately as the white bearded elder.

Sweet Potato Night, sweet, rooted and returning.

THE MINER'S VIEW

"She'll be coming round the mountain," a singing round does go. This modern travel with Airstream attached, can keep the song moving along. Melodies rise with the mountain crests, and rolls on down the other side. Follow a river in Pennsylvania and find a miner's view. Retired to a porch colored by age, rocking a chair bent on a tilt. Wrinkled a face peering from rocker to now. The man has spent life and breath of his own to bring depths deposit to surface and earn. Life in the earning while living was held in shafts and corridors of miner's darkest hour.

Into the light returned this form, air to breath from nostrils ladened. Sneeze at the change but none came free—this man living above, but the depths remain within the body. The air penetrates but black lungs cling, and eyes squint with uncertainty of his purpose, past, present and future remaining. The miner's wife came not to the porch, but on up the road a woman of another family was represented. She stood in mother hubbards dress of length, and two small children seeking skirts security. Hair matted at the end of the day from wind, rain and without a comb.

Miner's view closeted by the mountains, restrained by this condition, and unchanging except for the river beside. New places for our eyes to greet, smile, wave and time rolls these wheels away. Have we hurt those who saw us come, and drive on past? Did hearts reach out and seek an escape upon the silver wheels of our Airstream flying?

Wind up the valley and ponder awhile—they gave us warmth in era before atoms. Have these men wondered if the moon were to be mined and searched for mineral? Has the miner dreamed of up, up and away my gold mine in the sky? Does miner's view afford him dreams or have dreams been left beneath the surface and the shaft of light never reached his destiny?

Miner, friend, you contributed today to bring the heart to your world too. Miners View, can you read of life beyond your walls and tunnels? Another mountain upon another day, someone will drive by your rocker and wonder where have all the faithful gone?

Gone with the train whistle in the hollow, skimming past the timothy uncut and nodding goldenrod. Rocking chair and miner on the tracks of life and train running still on tracks built by man. While fog is illusive and knows no tracks to follow. Miner's view, have you found philosophy and theology to mix with your geologic strata? Has light from the mask penetrated and widened the valley between mountains and thought?

THE LAURENTIAN DRAMA

Just up Brier Hill, down from Sweet's Corners there's a sign that says, "Bunny's Home," all along the way in Ontario. Following through the Laurentian chain where only outcroppings remain and rolling hills once mountains of oldest acclaim. Riding down the King's Highway of Englishman's design and in Canada a dominion that's so fine.

Tall brown cattails along a blue-green swamp, like plumes upon hats of Royal Guard. Raindrops signal the coolness of wind to rustle the blue delphium of a lady's garden. The sky draping down in storm biding like weeping willow boughs beside a windmill broken.

An hour off the International Bridge at Thousand Islands you'll find that gravel roads and dust can be a camper's choice. Move along slow and turn to the left just before two ruts up ahead. Drive in a lane echoing with thunder like a stereo encore before the concert. Stop at the house for box seats beside a majestic stone house in hand hewed glamour. First night at a premier and bouquets beside the stage in marigold splendor. The white lace curtains with a french beauty falls in myriads of folds upon a white sill. Beside the driveway grape leaves bow and fruit of the vine so small.

Patience follows the gravel way and at the old house corner, a lake magnificent for a whole setting unfolds. The rain sprinkles down and little sizzles burst on the hickory-fire while smoke curls up toward the Ontario night. Beauty and rain, peace like a lake is running full.

The scene is a camper's paradise being washed in rain and clover grows in the country here. The Laurentian night melts away and finds its resting place.

EVERGREENS OF RIDEAU

Lake Rideau in Ontario Province is recognized for size and beauty even on a relief map sculpture. Beyond Thousand Islands town, lies this well of open beauty. No cap to seal it, no pump to drain it dry, and on the lakescape stands the Evergreens of Rideau.

Those Evergreens stand in clusters like a family, growing up toward the sky, from tall to small. Wind, rain, and snow must call to the trees but they wave in return and keep their vigil. Lush green grass and clover thrives in the meadow surrounding this chosen niche.

Lake Rideau survives the storm rolling across, and chants its own lapping reverie. While the evergreens listen and find the rain their daily bread.

Man draws pictures to bring a view into the home for containment. So artists paint great strokes of green and blue. While another writes what eyes and words grasp as description—yet other eyes may see it differently. Each to his own heart and choice, while Evergreens of Rideau change into Chritsmas trees standing twelve feet high.

Song of the birds, carols in the heavens, beside a lake being refilled. Nature seems to be the receiver of eternal replenishment, while man scoffs at so much of a thought.

Great giant drops of rain sting against the windowpane. Each forming its own tributary into a puddle flowing toward the evergreen feet. Amidst a lake of ever change, thunder rolls and skies open to see a tree studded horizon across the watery miles. Skies dip low and the scene is erased, except for brains now clear recall. Gone the horizon of far evergreen, gone the lake of ebbing waters. Gone with the storm and shore returns. The sky unfolds again and the view is fragmented in an instant of fog. No scene remains in unchanging plan. Nothing can be forever the constant same. Moving, moving man senses this, but his movement alone obscures his knowledge that God is forever moving in this dimension of life. Man tries to move the mountains, search the seas, soar to the planets, while a Cosmonaut once declared, "God wasn't up there!" God is everywhere showing his delicate inscription to his creative countenance. Yet man says, "It's thunder, lightning, another storm."

Sermonettes aren't needed in this sanctuary with cathedrals chiming above. This moment of now is clear like the lake that wisdom is given each individual when time is taken for a quiet moment in isolation to world, and open communication only toward heaven.

Evergreens of Rideau, light changes your color to new shades of green. The shadows bring out design to your enchanting branches. The shadows of experience brings out your design and enchanting pattern for continued growth. Parallels upon a page like the lake horizontal. While Evergreens of Rideau point the direction for faith. Walking upright in vertical position, seeking God's Hand is outreach of condition. Evergreens of Rideau—time and place—thank you too!

LAKE RIDEAU
Ontario, Canada

TRANS-CANADIAN

Split rail fences criss-cross the countryside. Brown cattails with silver green leaves creep through the swampy lowlands. Quiet shores of the Rideau River watch lilies upon the water and sleepy boats anchored. Evergreens beauty comes in elegant grace among skirts of frosty fog.

A Providence away, birch bark is found stemming tall, and papery thin. White the skin and skimming in shadows against a forest of mixed chapparel. Bouquets of blackeyed susans growing in roadside clump like vases. All this along The King's Highway motion. Home of the Maple Leaf, a visitor's sight and a Trans-Canadian vacation.

Fleet the hours like a French waitress serving. Food as cuisine as a gourmet on Sunday, while mixed in a recipe of food for thought.

Ottawa, Capital of a country so large, and above the architecture chimes rang crystal clear across the early morning. Fountains bursting in petals of molded metal and churning down in splattering rhythm. Chimes, cathedral, and flags out flurled, a heart of a nation was in seconds achieved. Serious folk, with strains of Old World tradition built at the top of the steeple and cone.

Pointe-Fortune or Montee' Wilson Nord, towns crossing roadway before mountains Laurentian ahead. Tent like shapes dot the field of hay and shaped by hand, let it dry today. Rows of corn in trenches of water across the fields toward Nord or Sud.

Roads at the sign, man at attention, while life on the move in his own monastery. Pinnacles of direction point the change in view. Sun hidden from Sundays name as Fleur de leis glows in symbol. Montee' Lavigne your French towns name, gilded in letters and flurl ensue.

Quest the direction from whence we came. Est on the way toward, while Nord lies to the left, and Sud our own way home. This is land of our neighbor's nation and silver times steeped in enchanting Trans-Canadian lore.

While sails blow in the northern winds and dotted against islands in the sunset.

FRENCH TOAST

Frying french toast in a skillet of accent, would be difficult in ingredients, without the fire. So goes breakfast in French Canadian country where eyes speak universal language of agreement or so. Where language runs different in tongues enunciation, while wave of the hand says farewell you know. French toast morning in liquid for frying, while rain mixes in wind and leaves clothes for drying.

Yonder electric generators send out its element against grey skies with wires and a splash of sun. Miniature the shadow with gigantic rumble, as passenger train races in vibrating rhythm. Away to the city of Montreal with skyways and highways in modern array. "EXPO" remains from elegant display and countries architecture portray.

Blue, orange, yellow, and green banners whisper in a fine color toward farther north. Into far country a mountain range pierces the mist and cliffs of original rock seen above a french toast plate. Farm buildings dot the countryside in quest of the soil. To raise the corn to mill for bread, and on to feed the breakfasting masses. Mild cheddar cheese of soft yellow hue is tangy, sharp and marvelous too. The herds that supply from pastures green, all feed on continents plentious same. French toast morning, with a buttery richness while waiting for sun to dry the syrupy rain.

Clover blossoms for honey blooming, without the bees to search each one. Blue minature bachelor buttons to deck a vase upon the table. The board is spread upon this table earth, what prayers are given for such a bounteous day?

The day is begun, and fed so well in physical food for breakfast time. While morning blessings filled the heart and capturing a moment among the French. Toast so simple, and people in too their taste, but their lace curtains speak of Old France's decor.

French Toast Morning finished too soon, but look for the day between the curtains and shade. A la French!

NOSTALGIA'S RETURN

An island named after a patron saint lies surrounded by the channel and to find it is to come by ferry in a very old custom of wait. Come over the brow of a hill, the view is caught in spellbound little islands surrounding, with tall pines watching, and a few seagulls watch the fisherman laze in the liquid media. Gravel roads skirt the island and cross one lane bridges closely. Cabins dot the hills sparsely from the owners short summer visit.

Sun of the afternoon caught an old milk separator holding a lawn planter's view of geraniums and petunias as fresh as the air of the islands own beauty.

Memories have returned to visit and find a lonely old cabin where a boy came with his family to fish and relax. The sky frames the background of the dominion of red maple leaf. There has been so little change of two decades, the people age, the land settles down, each winter takes its own due time, the buildings weather and match the calm. There's no real hurry for tomorrow, until today.

While waiting for the ferry that is unhurried, a bridge is being built and isolation will leave as the last trestle is in place. Cut the ribbons for a grand opening, and the island will suddenly become a haven for the tourist and where have all the old-timer's gone?

Return in hand with a piece of yesterday a little monument to youth. The rock upon which this island stands is now our own souvenir, before there's a change. Change will come from free ferry to toll bridge, but will the roads of time change the pace of the wilderness country way?

Stand on the edge of the island and there's a little white lighthouse—the ferry is coming, the sky looks like a bit of rain to moisten the dust of yesterday.

The stopover has been grand and we have been blest by the best of all—the time to stop and see anew. Renew, refresh and sparkle as the blue waters ebb, up to an island with seven sentinels called the Canadian pine.

Too soon we'll cross through the customs house, and lose this savor of another nation's gift. A gift of retreat of quiet changeless islands dotted against a mainland that's alive too!

ST. JOSEPH ISLAND
Ontario, Canada

THE WILDERNESS SPEAKS

Morning's crispness matches the freshness of the wilderness fern still basking in the edge of shadow. The clearing is only a small entrance of this far north country that has held the adventurous and hopeful in its strong lure.

The tall tree country far beyond Canada's border hemline is the wide open view of blue sky, spires of pines as high as the view and sparkling lakes crystal clear in untouched change.

Where a meadow is the crossroads of moose on the way to a rewarding lakeside drink and splash. There's a gravel fire road just yards uphill that shows the yet moist tracks of a fleet deer enroute with hurry, sharp toenails of a raccoon out to explore, and the lumbering gate is matched by the stride of a bear with tracks so broad to cast them would be a chance to meet face to face.

This blue sky country that dreamers seek is high in the finding if you drive as far as you can, and meet a sign that says, "End of the road." It's no construction intent, the instructions are clear, there's a land without change except by the slow ebbing of the wave of wind, generations and a need to search for farther frontiers.

So here on a morning with a window steamed and tiny dewdrops widening, the view outside is one of freshness; quiet except for all the call of natures own step, and loveliness as strong as the timbers, as deep as the sky, as blue as the waters, as sparkling as the sun that laughs on the lakes, green as the fern with little pointed arrow tips, and alone with those thousands of miles of silence.

May threshold of tomorrow not creep too fast into this virgin land, as already the mark has taken the Indian away. He lingers in the romanticism of our age old beliefs, but culture has swept him into the change and now he's apart of today's own strength.

Roam these inlets, climb these hills, search for the headwaters in birch canoes of heritage. This is their story with pages unread, and may someday their folklore be the song of these waters, the beauty of these forests, and the magnitude of the blue sky widening. Yet they speak with their eyes—have you ever noticed?

But the road goes on. . . . .   BEYOND NORTH BAY
                                        Ontario, Canada

EXPLORING THE WOODS

There is a hill that slopes up and meets the low brush in greeting. The hill shares the day with wild red raspberries ripening and not far away a bear holds a hidden retreat.

Yesterday the bear's giant tracks were cast in a mold and let to dry. He came so near his odor mixed with the forest and made us hurry. The casts are his past in step with our moving today, away to a city desk for a far off reminder. A bit of yesterday and today is taken along, as we pack to depart from this far north country. This land of the great Canadian Woods is filled with beauty, splendor and a song of its own.

The songbirds are few this late summer day, as fall is progressing and they must hurry away. The hearty remain like snowshoe rabbits, whose brown of the late summer is a rich coat indeed, but change of the seasons and they are part of its array.

Birchbark gleams in the sunshine and curls in the wind. The leaves speak in rustling words and seem to have a message of sharing these days to have been for purpose and never despair.

There's wood for a fire tonight at dusk, for whomever comes. There's a spider web shimmering in the sun like a silver line across a picnic bench, it all beckons for another return.

The road grader creeps down the hill and smooths away the ruts, away with the rocks, and tracks of man. The giant wheels move like a noisy bear, but the engine breaks the spell of silence.

A mosquito returns to look at the intruder of man at his table and is caught in the web.

To sit in the sunshine, and long to return. To dream in the daytime, and to rest in the night. This is the story of the far norths own hamlet. It's filled with the beauty of lakes sharing the land, by their own making, and stay on and on.

This is God's Country, and preserve it we must. It's for all of those to cherish the fresh, the rugged, and search for its beginning. Search for a threshold you need never go any further, for it's here in the country, untouched by any hurry. The flurry of seasons is all it has need.

Tall pines, white birch, and wild raspberries we'll leave you here, for heat of the city would make you wilt and die.

Return for a re-creation of living afresh—we'll cherish this moment and yearn for another view—cross over the swinging bridge—it has its own thrills!

FROM THIS VALLEY

Among the New Hampshire lands there crests a moment of quiet beauty. Where white butterflies cross a flowing river in magic speed. Where eyes look up and find towering mountains in majesty purple.

A well worn path beside the waters from rapids above. Surmising a fishermans haven among this meadow surveyed by birch and evergreen. Petals of daisies greet the footsteps waving. A signal to stop and pick these beauties of the wild nature scene. Tall calendulas of amber and gold are wildly growing and bidding too. While tall evergreens, like choir robed singers await the conductors wand. The forest surrounding this river of music is peace beyond the river. Sun squints through the powdery clouds and warms the day with bells of chiming happiness.

On a far road, vehicles accelerate and miss the crackling of natures steps, and bird's throaty song. Breaking this quiet in man's busy life is a plane above winging across the view. Too high to see, except for patterns of blue, green and gold. Clover purple misses the fragile focus in far distance, or pebbles under feet in slow motion.

Last year's growth lies brown upon the ground, while this year's harvest presses up from seeds sown. Gather the daisies and count the petals. Gather memories and count the memories. Gather the basket held with blessings, all this in a summer moment among these New Hampshire hills. These mountains of purple glory and everlasting beauty.

From this valley carries up a pine scent and rolling harmony. The battery of human strength must be checked for dry cells, and adding water for soul's regeneration. While pine winds blow, and birch bark glistens.

WIDE OPEN COUNTRY

Climb away roads toward homesteads, farmsteads, and roll past all. Winding roads repeat the turn and crosses a bridge from highlands run off. Lanes curl up like a pencil drawing and no freeways haunt this paradise in maple syrup country.

Birch bark drying peals away thin, and leaves a untouched skin and grain. Pine logs simmer in spicy condition while fireplaces crackle at the warmth of a hint. Home cooking tastes eloquent from a skillets container and ham simmering beside mountains of potatoes. Gravy creamy to alamode the plate, while side dishes crave another helping. Oven warm from home baked pie all this in wide open country. A touch and taste of spice comes from an old lamp two tier bubbles high. This light of antique fashion and shining upon the linen tablecloth with fringe.

Fringes of time, tinges of picture, sketches of color, and hearts respite. Next door a family who belong to us, with open door and welcome mat. Wide open times for fun and play. Dinners spread, guests at places, and thanksgiving said before partaking all. Times lit upon brightest face in happiness shared. Wide open country, this our own, where land of thy birth rings loudly clear. Citizens born, citizens above, come passing generations in the march toward ultimate.

Open country wide this place to walk alone and find it filled with moments to cherish, and take away. Camera films the moving events, hearts compact the living experiences and minds cherish the completeness.

Completeness of being upon a second, is conscious awareness to nearness of God. God of this land, peace of this moment, eternal this second, transforming smallness into greater purpose.

Eyes drinking in the wide open country with love. Love of home upon the move is roots stronger and boundless in measure. No measure this day to express it's time, no cup could hold this happiness found.

Wide open country thy cup runneth over in beauty and blessings. How great thy majesty of country have you found?

SCENIC MAINE SIXTEEN

Meadow larks flying along the roadside just after entering. From New Hampshire the wheels left behind and joined
the winding roads through birch groves of appealing white
bark. Crossing a bridge, the third to hold the now silent
river at Wilson's Mills, west. On through the Aziscoos
Mountain a raging river with rapids pulsating and water
churned into white falling foam. Movies chasing the water
with the press of a button. The highway stopover seemed like
an Olympia Rainforest with feather fern and confetti mist.

At Deer Mountain Lodge overlooking a lake of its own,
finds a tree bent as an Indian marking his former path. Log
roads cut forests into fractions while highway is notched in
wrinkled folds. Like a black forest, the timber untouched
by saw, or sun's laser beam. Just over a ridge set against
green is a tiny valley where the sun catches a brown cattail.

Wild strawberry plants amble freely right up to the
stalks of wild phlox with blooming lavender stars. An ava-
lanche burst down upon Highway 26 last night and closed
its travel and brought Route 16 into our travel day. Pine
and tar seep into the air as road is dotted now with the black
patch repairs.

Scenic Maine Sixteen brought traveler to visit with a
friend and renew old friendships. All this among the summer
greenery and long gone winter's skiddoo trails. No skiddos
cross the terrain in July, but fog can climb as high as the
snowbanks of winters former touch.

Maine so scenic on sixteen, and stop again on Main Street, where Constable and citizen will agree it's a fine place to be.

DIRECTION OF NIGHTMARE

In land where roads lack signs of name and direction-drive with verbal directions to aid a Samaritan. Intentions were good but only complete in half and wayfarer lost by twos. Down the road and directed to turn left again but no sign to destination. Taking man's directions blindly and mixed with frustration of so far off the mainstream of travel.

So haunt the dusk with fog enveloping above first cranberry bogs, ponds and greater lakes it seems. A sign deep into swamp country and no place to turn the clock back to day. Forging ahead with six tons on now gravel roadbed, and tearful frightened eyes of the navigator. Edging onward, now following arrows toward a campsite advertised so finely the travelers best. The roadbed gravel oozed with stones, mud and sinkholes too. The approaching night gave a last quick nod to day and in that second between the inlets of water which were seemingly held by fence and levee, standing above mocking a road and traveler.

Square lights were seen from campers windows mixed the trees of darkness. No pole lamps beside this lake encompassing, and great anguish of fright retreated to safer distance.

At last to stop on solid ground, too soon after drenched in storm. Quiet the fears, with home's welcomed walls and aromas from the stove to give reassurance. Nightmare in the dark, like coffee without cream, while soup in the vegetables bubbling cauldron. Night light attached to a bulb and plug makes a birch bark trunk look like a rising candle.

Thankful that a prayer was answered and now a child says, "the soup's smell run high" in the pangs of hunger. Feed the lambs and put to bed, and given an extra hug that dreams aren't real in a nightmare, only those in the driving night without direction, sign and assurance of safety. Directions of nightmare from vertical thought in subconscious sleep, but horizontal traveling with water surrounding, bring light of day to prove it less adventurous.

Pilgrims how brave you really were! While noodle soup fills the bowl like logs floating away. Nightmare leaves with the flick of a switch and there was light.

CANTEEN LIFE

Avid tenters and one vent trailers abound this doorstep view. Chasing mosquitos bigger than flies and sunrise edging in through the fog. Neatly set the wooden picnic tables and shelves piled high with kitchen provisions outside. Women vacationing away from it all? No beauty shops to cascade the locks, no homely joys of washer and dryer. But there's trees, fresh air and a lawn someone else cares for.

Cars splashed with states of mud, but even here the male of pride lets it stay. There's a river he's hankering to call his own if for a catch or two. Children still sleeping— so no bees swarm wild, and wild crows call has an echoing alarm. Patches of blue sky creep into view while fog domi- ates the lofty lot.

The canteen comes again to the water spiggot and re- fills. While another with a jerry jug there goes a green cup and knife and red wash basin too. A litter bug drops a hefty hand of trash into the tired green can, but exasperatedly remembers "don't" and bends in sprawling exercise. From the ladies room pops out the first yellow pair of pedal pushers bounding along with orange sash flying. First of the small fry have found the time to dress for the occasion. A boy lumbers out of a camper in brown plaid and looks at break- fast in hopeful glance. Some man is dressed in bathing suit the least to be concerned about and swim or fish it's his vacation.

Tree Number 48, is still the favorite beneath the green leaves. That's where the canteen is again refilled.

Out comes a jacket for a blonde lass of nine, while father gathers his cigarette and machette one at a time. Cigar smoke just woke the morning and no need to see its size. It's good to have watched this parade to the modern water well. Too often it's forgotten that the city dwellers from all around are striving for more than status and move from a one hatch vent to two or more. Here by coincidence, here by fate, another side of America's face was met at the well carrying the small canteen. All sizes of containers, to all strata of people, all seeking refreshment from their busy roads.

While clothes dry upon their draping lines, this ink can move on with the turn of a switch, roll of a wheel, and clock ticking on. It's breakfast time here and the hot water running. So lucky each to his own way and sight.

Canteen and well, life teems for more, while this cup runneth over and gallons to carry in a sealed tank. Shape of this vehicle like a MQF, it's a container too and wells up in an experience that keeps the canteen filled. "9161," glad you are all rigged to castoff for more sights and lives to touch in an instant of quiet eye. Canteen Life, water or words!

HIGH GO ON

At high go on, comes a feeling of sky so low. This tonight between two ranges in the Catskills. Three miles west by directions printed, yet none to say it's all going up. Climbing a lonely mountain road, and no place to turn around. That's high go on, etched in clouds so low. So sky so low ran beside the mountain and a ghost village laid in stillness. The houses stood and grass grew tall, doors closed and driveway barred. High and go on past a camp with cars parked all neat. Clean across the well washed camp not a soul to be seen, and a mile more to wind upwards. Heart in a flutter, eye on the road, while ears heard water racing off the mountainside.

A sign at last and High Go On no more than a turn. Stop and to park, but the array of people like Mother's windowed shoe. Long dark lashes, eyes flashing too, sleek profiles in the mist. And Humpty Dumpty came bursting from a wall. Here among these camping nooks came people of city born and bred, but back to the highlands like their ancestors of European line.

This paradise among the stars at High Come In. Ukaranian in name so quaint and friendly in the mountain of their kinship. Songs ring the evening like a league of nations in accented tongue. Listen carefully and the laughter is the same whatever the name.

High Come In, must now High Come Down, after High Go On had reached its destination of today and surprising in its sharp climb. Climb and descend a lesson in living. Do we understand the language or is it high go on and never stop?

MYSTIC MORNING

Morning dawned in the Catskill highlands. Again upon celluloid film was a locked door, and ornate bannisters. Detect again an instinctive note upon the scale of musical isolation. Up a lane walked an elderly man pushing a bicycle with a small bag of sticks and grass. Old World from where did you come? Too quickly gone by to catch his wrinkled face or dim eyes of once a peasant. What ethnic cult has haven sought and found in this secluded spot?

A colony of bungalows seemed deserted yet again autos stood without a hum. Upon a moment, time and eyes stopped and there upon a lodge balcony stood, "Yesterday." Yesterday, stood in a great white flowing beard and black garb draping his small form. In hand was held a book spread open like Saint Peter's entrance book. Three black garbed men in black wide brimmed hats listened. With backs so turned that invading noise stirred not their summoned presence. Another came walking to join his three, while eye was forced on, by time, place and space.

Small children flocked in a country courtyard and where and why to understand. Forests posted, "No Trespassing Allowed," while mystery persists at this unique kind. Old traditions alive in attempt to preserve a culture by isolation? Have they found their Promised Land, or are they waiting to return to their Israel?

Stimulating thought from emigration to immigration and which way the tide? Resort upon reflection or displacement upon inquiry. Above the city in mountain hamlet an unexpected rendezvous with a Mystic Morning.

To inscribe the location would bring their isolation to a close and why not let the mountain hold their secrets, and cliffs hold the remnants?

Mystic Morning within the Catskills—you still remain.

Chapter V

TAKE TIME FOR THE LITTLE THINGS

THRESHOLDS IN MOTION

Wind, sun and sea mix here beneath the pier. The winds of fall race with gusty surge. The sun is hidden in whipcream drops and pushes aside the clouds with wind, fresh cheeks blushing. The sea ripples in and lashes the sandbar into its own boxed in container. The wild ducks seem to have chosen the high winds to hurl them toward another sunny spot beside the sea.

The sheltering trees of summer whisper farewell to warm winds. Boats adieu to the river, their answer to warnings of the tide and sea. Planes aloft loom like sea gulls poised before their landing on the land beside the sea.

Sweet calls of autumn has lured the home fires to kindle and air now holds sweet pungency from another woods, lake and land. Children's voices no longer race ahead of feet toward the pier. All those voices have left the call of their own wild urges, and gone to sit so quietly. Their ears hear the call of wind and hearts beat faster for greater release to climb with the wind and feel this beat. While winds go echoing across the rushing waters. Be still and stop your daydreaming dears, there's other lessons planned and freshness in learning for your lives to live.

Great mountains of the sea, wind and land can we climb them all and be the same? To be unchanging is untaught. For growth is built in the ever moving, ever new, ever greater heart. The pulse races on with the beating waves, the brain refreshed for the winds that erase the smog of stagnation and growth begins another climb for the summits.

Summit each day at the peak of awareness, and plateau's in comprehension with the Spirits empowering grant. Reach for the heights by Christ's own hand; in nearness to steady the step, in nearness for wisdom, and nearness that erases the aloneness at many thresholds.

Thresholds of living so adventurous in the new frontiers yet unexplored in philosophical planes. Reach on toward the mountaintops in highest grandeur and find this life being lived within the motion of beauty, the emotion within, and devotion amplified toward God of All.

THE RAGGED EDGES

The ragged edges of the grey carpet is being flung about. It seems to rise right up and be shaken aloft. This grey Persian weave, vertical, horizontal, and diagonal too. The snapping grey clashes, rolls and snaps in great elastic jerks. It swells and whips in the rising winds, this great grey carpet in masters immensity. It canopies out and rises too, high like another Aladdin's famous ride. Up over the top of a lighthouse at day, swinging, crashing in electrical charge. Leaves crash as the edges tear, birds are lost in its greyness now. Sweeping, past in racing terror, this carpet swells, and takes its claim. It's lighted by so high a power, trembles in the torrent pelt. Lashing, smashing those ragged edges unwoven at last.

Stringy wet like a soggy rope that's tangled, frayed and scored. The ragged edges lift a tiny bit with the air now passing into brighter skies. Would you believe those ragged edges that raged was the giant clouds above, just awhile ago?

TICK-TACK-TOE

Tick-tack-toe upon the window screen came the rain. The drops ran down like a woven print and drops rest. Splashes hit the screen and upon the windowpane. Jarred for a second when lightning and thunder met and shook this old house.

Softly the call of nature returns and plays tick-tack-toe upon the sand. The thrush spring out for a worm or two. The cardinal flits a cocky eye, while grey squirrel shakes his finery and races up to find a dinner nut. Tick-tack-toe with the rain, the thunder plays her roll, while lightning changes place and erases the small game.

The shrubbery hangs out limb and vine to dry upon its branchy line. The butternut tree in canopy between green and gold of a summer gone. Oh who hurried this game along and whisked the leaves upon the ground too soon? The grass takes heed to the latest drink and reaches for more. While man opens windows and watches for suns return. Tick-tack-toe the plane descends and finds his landing strip. All play their game of life while children dress up and make believe adults are the luckiest yet.

The wind plays her part just now and dries the screen print. The window dries and the drops still stay in spots. The birds dry out and fluff their wings, squirrel finds his feast, the plane finds its runway ready, children prance on, and the tick-tack-toe is almost gone, but a falling curtain took its play, and now the work begins again. The rain returns—all must stop—for she's the best in tick-tack-toe.

RAINDROPS & SHADOWS

Raindrops splashing and caught upon the locks dampened and gone. Have you ever seen the shadow of a raindrop? Light penetrates the eye and make things that were invisible visible and then we are satisfied. But for all things visible we must have forgotten to look for the invisible until a moment when the absence of light within, rain between the light beyond, and suddenly upon a wall the shadow of rain flows down the wall like grossgrain ribbon, and caught upon this paper a strange flowing river gravitated on its way.

Like heat waves that can't be contained, neither can these patterns of shadow but when the heart and soul are attuned then the eye is able to translate the view into meaning and on into significance.

A flashlight broke through the darkness defacing the pattern, and the univolt defunct caused this experience to be realized. There is a meaning for all, and the rain goes on, cold, wet and alone in the Gulf night.

Elated awareness, wearing and spent the day is gone, but still the rain on forest roof and a door slides closed and the lids of eyes close their thin veil, between night and day, dark and light, factual and ethereal. So ends the shadow but it rains the same.

THE FABULOUS FIG

When that fascinating fig and I first met it was ladened well with tiny green marbles. And the marbles grew and was admired by many. Just before ripening—away we sped for vacation and wondering who would pick the figs.

Home in a short time to find it neatly cared and tended. Still green figs growing and the ripe ones gone. One day before the typewriter, but no time to interrupt, for here was the answer to the mystery of a fig tree.

Just about noon when all was dry, I met the youth of the new brood of summer. The mockingbird daintly nibbled and enjoyed her feast from a limb just above a fig. A rusty thrush skipped in and proclaimed a morsel too—what a gorgeous luncheon all juicy and fresh. Along came a pair of twin little wrens, to enjoy a branch and hop back and forth. A smart silver trimmed black starling came in a flourish and gobbled his share with no manners at all. The starling squabbled with his twin, and I wished him away with the snap of my pen.

The cardinals flew in on a trip from the pear tree and enjoyed a lunch all shady too. They've all gone off on a wing and a song, except for a robin who's still running around. Nectar of a fig, vintage of delight—wonder if it was a peck too much?

A fig cup hangs partially sipped, while fall breezes hold it for another cardinals tasting. They're eating the figs just one at a time and almost ten have come to find. No figs for jam I understand. I'll just have to have peanut butter instead!

SUMMER LEAVES

The pear leaves falling signal the summer to close. Curling brown forms of stillness lie beneath the tree, feet and chair. Dark branches holding forth in sway between summer seasons turn to fall. Even the butternuts begin to change to golden parcels, where, oh where are you going so soon?

Only yesterday the baby birds were nodding beneath your leafy foliage—they've gone too. The sun seems to hover in the clouds of uncertainty between heavy rain and the comforting shower. Those August leaves are crispy crisp, and little brown shoes are worn too as summer leaves. Little fingers have made a doll of yarn and sits upon a washcloth throne. Off goes child, doll for a last summer stroll, down the grey steps echoing, scuff the heels, around the house, off to dream by the riverside. Off to the pier to feed the wild ducks born here this season. Too soon they'll find the instinctive call and lift their wings as summer turns. The tall swamp grass whistles softly and a gust upwelling sends a story off with its title.

The ducklings talking in twittering tones grabs the bread for an early dinner. The minnows grab for the slices too and great schools converge upon a quarry. The jellyfish race toward its magnetic pulse and sun finds a golden spot upon the ducks, water and reeds. The sky lifts its wings to hurry as a helicopter crosses its own great heaven.

Little barefeet race away through the summer grasses on her way toward its closing days. The minnow school is now their interest before their own is tolled.

119

The apples turning red, nod, bob, and fall and punctuate this hour. Soft warm breezes disappear while faraway ocean swells bring color notes, and the tide of a season turns.

Go again to the beach to say farewell, feed the ducks once more, pick up the pears and apples too. Summer leaves, but a soft breeze reminds of her return following the cycle and her call again. Those Autumn Leaves you are so enchanting as summer leaves and crickets call.

GROUND CHERRY FEVER

Where ground cherries grow there's a golden autumn pie.

Searching for those small golden gems brought eyes to follow a silver web. Down past the butternut clusters still attached. Out from beneath the crispy leaves all fallen, out past the apples in fresh aroma of sun and wind. Out to the country where gardens are calling harvest baskets to come. Inside the garden beyond the wooden fence, there's a warm smell of the ground, earth's own sweet perfume. There nestled under tiny bushes near the potatoes, are those golden ground cherries lying. The small cherries filled with millons of seeds are waiting for tender fingers to pick them and fill a small pail. There's never enough for a filled winter can, but pies of autumn you are worth a golden nugget. The crust will hold the cherries and sweet sugar juices bubbling, while eager mouths await that childhood treasure house of taste.

The garden is gone, and the cherries no longer are tended, lost beneath a tractors wheel and a newcomers busy furrow. An old man at the fruit stand looks shocked at the ground cherry request. Those lingering words seem a decade upon decade behind. So ground cherries of youth picked by another generation is gone. Unless hidden and preserved by some family out in the country somewhere. The sunny days are here again and wind returns to blow the corns now drying stalks. The whispering stalks nod farewell to summer, and offer their harvest to wagon arriving.

The corn to the grainary, the wheat is silent now, all tended, harvested and preserved. Autumn winds and golden ground cherry sun warms the gates that are swinging to a close. The pumpkins are glowing like Indian fires before tepee homes. Those memories long ago, when America was so young.

Ground Cherry Fever will leave with the tide and replace itself with other precious moments from beyond the turn of time.

NATURE'S HUE

On quiet steps beneath wild canarys flight, heart tilts upward and glides toward a filmy cloud. Clouds playing tag as the northeasterly blows, just like squirrels at play on butternut twigs. Each are reality focused on by the eye, and witnessed from a tiny fragment of world at the doorstep.

Pyracantha changes costume from royalty green to pumpkin glow before her crown reaches true and shiny red her throne. Color forever before eyes that share in beauty of moment, nature and a cornerstone of creation.

Mockingbird grey, a suit of fabulous finery was unsurpassed upon her jaunty line. While jays called out from blue feathers pierced with royal blue esthetic package that crayons never quite convey. Bobwhites call enthrall the ear, from this tiny spit between river and city. All in our own little lane of the country. An old cedar standing ready for winters reign and is flecked greener in cooler temperatures now.

Sirens never erase natures pure afternoon tones, but sun beckons to find a still leafy nest to rest. While pecan leaves rustle in her green and golden dress, the bark is clearer, and the leaves will flutter like birds on the wing.

Sun on the fence casts shadows like pictures frame too small, too large and what wall to fit? The roses have passed their tall throaty vases of loveliness and gained new space before cuttings begin. The lane is crushed gleaming crystal flecks. Golden in the afternoon sun, and radiating out a path for the homeward families return.

How beautiful this harvest upon the eastern step and land just beneath the eastern skies from the seas that spring. Rise up little clouds and carry the day in crystal perfection of color toward the western sunset.

All color of earth can never be matched but only in a replica for all in a sunset is the Creator's brush. Swirls in the clouds, rainbows in light and beauty held but for a moment in eternity.

CREPE MYRTLE SKY

Crepe Myrtle in bloom across this Virginia City lifts lavenders heavenward and signs its initials. The lacy blooms sway in the evening breeze and faint perfume haunts the way.

The cyclists witness the roof top silhouettes against the sky and wonder who lives just inside. Tall the homes with a two story flourish that appear above the crepe myrtle trees. Just on down about halfway, two hex signs shout of a travelers choice, and new cars parked in front of fences just above the wharf. Boats are resting on lawns sleepily, while sea gulls dip down to inspect.

Lazy thoughts and weary legs the cyclist meander down another Crescent Street. On toward home as the sky beckons to the changing sea. The crickets are hopping in shrubbery growth, while locusts chime, wail and disappear.

Crepe Myrtle Sky has gone away like a lovely gown packed away. The dusk is gathering and hazy azure creeps up on the evening. The last click of the screen door closes for today and voices seem to settle at the end of day.

Crepe Myrtle loveliness, pink and lavender has been put away and Norfolk is still awake.

SPIRALING BEAUTY

The winding, spinning, spiraling instant, went silently on its way. Light from afternoon sun's visit returns from the water to the boats glimmering shine. The swoop of a bird toward a moment, alighting like a sudden apple releasing its stem with the signal of the wind. Shadows dancing on a Sunday in Autumn and bring men to watch a boat drifting away.

Those spiraling leaves haunt the lawn at dusk and speak enchantment beneath a slippered foot. Between the branch and ground their release is a many splendored figure.

Like a child searching for the cookie cutters to make a delicacy in dough. All have a motion, and a time of its own. A moment in a season and a year again until Autumn. Like old-fashioned dumplings when fresh from the oven the spiraling splendor of aroma in action.

Hint of the beauty surrounding life is like the sweet flavor of vanilla. Just a trace for tasting in a recipe, yet spoonful would be bitter and the zest lost.

The timer rings and the baking is done, frost calls and summer is gone. While in between the golden hues there's spiraling beauty before the changes come. Just between Autumn and Winter and other seasons to create, there's Spiraling Beauty in the moments that slip into the Soul and remain forever yours.

NEARER THE CHIMES

The chimes of evening just before six, peal notes so clear, crystal and pure upon the air of evening. Distance lengthens its echoing refrain. Silence before a new thought rings and soul above the water moves with the rippling tide.

Three ducks on the golden wing of suns embrace break the tones with chatter. While a dove flies toward the sound, and a seagull rises a little higher. Minnows flash in the shadows.

A red boat rushes by and hears only its throating voice and the chimes didn't ring. An ivory handled knife lost in child's crabbing net on a summer day—found this evening while chimes pierced the day and small eyes found the knife in the channel of darkness. Pleading calls to the wild ducks brought them after the chimes sweet close. Nibbles of bread brought two by two, like beginning of the ark, and the ducks came too.

The chimes fed the heart with music of sweet peace, the feeding of the ducks brought song to the child's lips, the lost knife brought a set to completion.

A day ebbs forth toward another and Nearer The Chimes has gone away until tomorrow—just about the same time, same channel and no interference. No static ruins this nook on the pier where air blows free, waters come and go—the fountain of life is refilled.

THE BUFFET OF AN ORGANIZATION

Flags of the Supreme Allied Command Atlantic decked the tables for lunch on a September noon for their ladies. The ladies came from their homelands represented by those affiliated with the great body of NATO SACLANT Headquarters, Norfolk, Virginia. This was the scene of a lovely luncheon of the Wives Club and an ice carving of eagle in flight an Admiral's gift of welcoming splendor. While lunch of buffet, all hots and colds, from United States ladies choice, while the eagles beak dripped in fluid rhythm.

Voices melted too in friendly tones and became these ladies dignity. Conservative dress in tasteful appeal was modeled by Norway, Netherlands, England, France and more. Accents flavored the food and conversation from homelands to vacations all spent. New faces from across the sea, new faces to meet from here to there. All this a stimulating moment upon the wings of a career made by an officer's billet and fashioned by invitation from the hostess' too.

A group of ladies who have lived around the world, traveled horizons far beyond wildest hopes and a stopping now to enjoy new presences, a new table of friendship and a cup of graciousness served with warmth. This is the graciousness of these ladies style and elegance in their personage not just in fashions seam.

Like the wings and swords all crossed upon a plaque that spells NATO SACLANT this is the spirit of unity from continent to continent and oceans of courtesy in between.

Insurance in policies that a salesman sells, but life and friendship is an insurance tangible. All this a blue and white star high above this special port at Norfolk, Virginia. A guest to be, a guest to stay and a moment shared today!

HOME

Home after a holiday away, where deep thoughts and entrance into mountains retreat gave the inner peace so often sought and to some never found.

In the heart of a meadow's grasses, where a fresh spring fed stream bubbled and spoke a cheery greeting before leaving the little bridge and cascade over rocks placed to hear its voice much stronger.

The babbling brook is still deep in the beauty of mountains strength, and the common things of life are perpetuated in genuineness. The beauty of it all is it came along home today. The freshness of sights have now become insights to dwell in the heart like the fresh spring for refreshment.

How lovely the meadow of changing carpet, it's here because contentment is its own quiet place. Home and the valley, home and the mountains, home and the sparkling of a summer nights eyes so bright—these eyes—the stars out there looking out and from home our eyes looking for the good that surrounds home and others.

The little country lane canary that flew just out of the reaching eye, was at least a promise that existence is often surrounding without the awareness because its just another set of fluttering wings.

When scripture speaks of every feather numbered and known relating to birds of the air, it suddenly means; like men today so many, we still are known, but its the accounting heart that recognizes the individual and not just another fluttering heart.

Home keeps us company, when other members have slipped away. But they return and so unexpectedly just like a little swallow that must have followed us home.

Loveliness is the never interrupting of thoughts just the joining in and like, "I just came out to tell you," of a child's happy voice.

Blue hydrangea that wilted in the afternoon has lifted up its blue round face to the evening dusk and seemed to say, "you noticed that we were waiting for your return to home."

There's a broken brick on the step that suddenly was missing, and hadn't been noticed before, isn't it grand to leave and return, and find even the little things are worth noticing?

Take a stroll with your thoughts to meadows, valleys and mountaintops rising above the busy life; then return and home no matter its rare size and condition it will be welcomed.

A door closes next door, and thoughts too have found a reverie hinge that there's time again to begin again and work will fly with the wings of another day.

Home, rest and all is best, because it spells, "So Blest!"

WAVES FOR YESTERDAY

Waves for yesterday splash against the shores of today. From seas around the the world, bows of a Mariner points the way.

Dugouts of size to smallness dished, spell mystery of time and when all this began. Time that the yearning of man matched the restless waves outside. So the fate of nations was chiseled, into outriggers, dugouts, canoes, and giant vessels too. From Mariner's strength to great atoms today and nuclear giants are in a docks great jaws.

Visit the Mariner's Museum of Newport News and a tour in Virginia's history is less than wrinkled and dry upon a parchments log. It's weathered and seasoned with ageless wares of the sea, and treasures retrieved by a scouting scuba. Figureheads hang in giant effigy to those great moments at the bow. When mist and waves splashed carvings into softer features and painted designs of religious art and seemed to grow into mellowed craft.

Places for men where once they sat, bronze skinned from sun or God's own hand. Islands in the Pacific, or England's far shore, all these treasures are at Mariner's door.

Even the wares of world and man, represented by strange torpedos that were guided by the hand of man. Walk those corridors, out near the bay, and take with you another moment when wind, rain and mist was shouldered silently by the boat and Mariner same.

132

Carvings keen, thoughts as vivid as the lighthouse glass that graces the central dome and catches the sun in refracted rainbow promise. Waves of light, waves of the sea, all mastered by man in skimming the blue. Changing horizons, and viewing the new, all dreams of more than the moment then. Waves of yesterday, locked behind silent doors tonight, and figureheads at the helm in motionless state. Silence, but for the clock, in changing of time on toward more waves of yesterday.

A PEARL MAYBE

Waves pour iridescent upon the Atlantic sands, like Pacific thunder too. In a place beside the sea the sands dip deep with barefeet prints and winds that move it onward. The sea oats dances in the wind like beige lace. Bouquets of it grow upon the dunes and wave against the sunset toward the westward sky.

There's a sight spectacular that few ever witness in the night. A giant strand of pearls glow in elegance with two clasps to hold it in its grandeur. Could anyone believe that upon an Atlantic evening dress, dance Chesapeake pearls? Not from oysters, but a manmade bridge going somewhere. Lights that glow upon midnight. The sounds pound around this harbors throat while lightship and pilotship stand guard and protection to voyaging.

The ocean pours ceaselessly, and lovers walk the sands, hand in hand against the din of waves and hearts pounding in happiness beat. Sea shells lie buried in their sandy bed tonight and erases even the evidence. Winds blow above the cypress gnarled and the dunes that lie in giant hills with seagrass sweeping. Sweeping the gaze toward the beautiful, beautiful sea and it drowns out the noises of the roaring crowds. The swelling sea oats, sea shells and granules of sand.

Great waves pouring ceaselessly is music like no hall of fame could contain. Sights are joys prepared for all who choose the paths they walk.

Worlds oyster in pearly glitter, remember it took many sands of time to bring its growth. Who dares to claim it for their personal own? Or is this sight a pearl of great beauty?

WINDS ACROSS THE WORLD

Winds across the world, from what land have you so recently crossed? What isle was your resting place, what slope your warming place? Did you touch England's foggy shores, or race up a Danish fiord? Or were you higher still and skipped across an Alp highland or two? Or did you make Holland's windmills dance and shake the storks nesting in chimney's nooks?

Winds across the world from continents far beyond, racing on toward the edge of this continent where sun is setting on our western shore. Or wind across the Pacific to lift and sweep and swell. Warm winds across the tropics, to natives own homes too. Winds across Australia and sheepherders call, or crossing the lands of Fuji's reign and land of Rising Sun. Across the Hong Kong that forever dries her clothes on balconies and on, and on, and on.

Where have the winds rested? Where has the air found freshness and like the restless sea is forever moving. Winds across the world tonight lighted not in this darkness, but racing on with energy that could break into much light. Skies so filled with clouds upon this eastern shore. Where are you going? Are you hurrying to yet the beginning?

Humanity across the world today in light or darkness where are you going too? Are you racing with the serious winds intent upon a destiny, or are you racing only a clock to continue its constant turn?

TIME ON THE TURN you have been such a fascinating experience in living. Now the pen can travel no faster than the hand it turns. The winds are hurrying us onward, upward and a JOURNEY INTO FULFILLMENT is beginning. TIME ON THE TURN, I bid a fond adieu.

M. J. SCOTT

CPSIA information can be obtained at www.ICGtesting.com
Printed in the USA
LVOW08s1229280715

447851LV00011B/27/P